T0194243

LETTERS TO CHRISTOPHER

Bringing Your Spiritual Journey
into Focus Through the Lens
of Your Family Stories

James K. Wagner

WESTBOW
P R E S S®
A DIVISION OF THOMAS NELSON
& ZONDERVAN

This book is a work of non-fiction. Unless otherwise noted, the author and the publisher make no explicit guarantees as to the accuracy of the information contained in this book and in some cases, names of people and places have been altered to protect their privacy.

NRSV: Scripture quotations are from the New Revised Standard Version Bible, copyright © 1989 the Division of Christian Education of the National Council of the Churches of Christ in the United States of America. Used by permission. All rights reserved.

CEB: Scriptures taken from the Common English Bible® (CEB). Copyright © 2012 by Common English Bible and/or its suppliers. All rights reserved.

MSG: Scripture taken from The Message. Copyright © 1993, 1994, 1995, 1996, 2000, 2001, 2002. Used by permission of NavPress Publishing Group.

WestBow Press books may be ordered through booksellers or by contacting:

WestBow Press
A Division of Thomas Nelson & Zondervan
1663 Liberty Drive
Bloomington, IN 47403
www.westbowpress.com
1 (866) 928-1240

Because of the dynamic nature of the Internet, any web addresses or links contained in this book may have changed since publication and may no longer be valid. The views expressed in this work are solely those of the author and do not necessarily reflect the views of the publisher, and the publisher hereby disclaims any responsibility for them.

Any people depicted in stock imagery provided by Getty Images are models, and such images are being used for illustrative purposes only. Certain stock imagery © Getty Images.

ISBN: 978-1-9736-3028-9 (sc)
ISBN: 978-1-9736-3030-2 (hc)
ISBN: 978-1-9736-3029-6 (e)

Library of Congress Control Number: 2018906706

Print information available on the last page.

WestBow Press rev. date: 08/01/2018

To children the world over who will soon be experiencing the challenges, wonders, mysteries, and blessings of life.

Contents

Foreword

I met my paternal grandfather only a handful of times. He lived in Nevada, and we lived in Oregon. During our occasional visits, Grandpa Seyfarth seemed unsure of how to let go of his strict German upbringing and relate to his two rambunctious granddaughters. In fact, I don't ever recall having had a conversation of length with him as a child. However, when I visited him once as a young adult, it was as though a spigot had been opened, and all the stories he'd previously held back came spilling out. He shared stories of his youth, his experiences in the war, his family history, and even a bit of his humor. I tried to remember the dates and memories as they flowed freely, but in hindsight I wish I had better known how to preserve this treasure of family stories that had been poured into my lap.

Jim Wagner has gifted us with a guide for how to preserve the treasure of our family stories. In *Letters to Christopher,* not only does he honestly and poignantly share his own treasured family stories with us, but perhaps even more important, he encourages us to share our own history as well. The appendices to these letters are packed with practical suggestions on how to create our own letter exchange between generations through conversations, note taking, or even video recordings.

There seems to be a recent resurgence of interest in genealogy: television shows such as *Finding Your Roots,* ancestry websites, and even DNA tests that track our genetic history. We long to learn more about who we are based on and where our family has been. Letters like these between Christopher and his granddaddy are a gold mine for future generations. We better understand our own sacred stories when we know and honor the sacred stories of the cloud of witnesses who have gone before us.

I hope and pray that *Letters to Christopher* will serve as an urgent call for us all to share our stories with one another while we can, and to store these intergenerational treasures as gifts to future generations. When my grandfather passed away at ninety-nine years young, many of his stories passed away as well. I wish that I had taken the time to gather these before he was gone. May we be inspired to build intergenerational bridges of recorded stories that will be gifts to us today as well as for generations to come.

Sharon Seyfarth Garner
United Methodist minister, spiritual director, retreat leader, and author of two books (*Praying with Mandalas* and *Mandalas, Candles, and Prayer*)

Prologue

It's only a bookmark, one of dozens that I have lodged within the pages of my books. Yet every time I hold this particular bookmark, I pause and am transported to my earliest family remembrances. Yes, it's only a bookmark—a very old one—but this one is special and raises unanswered questions.

The printed message reads, "A good book is good company."

The bottom of this slender piece of cardboard reads, "A souvenir of Key West, Fla."

On the reverse side, written in ink, it says:

Jan. 29, 1957

Mr. Albert Stone

N. Ft. Myers, Fla.

Mr. Albert Stone—that's my mother's father, the one all of us grandchildren called Granddaddy Stone. A hard worker all his life, he barely made enough to provide for his wife and four children. He did assembly line work in a blanket factory, with forty years' service before retiring. My cousins and I were not well acquainted with this man even though he was fully committed to his family. We do know his lifestyle was characterized by routine. All of us still refer to shredded wheat as granddaddy cereal because that was what he had for breakfast every day of the week.

I never pictured Granddaddy as an avid reader or lover of books. My hunch is that in January 1957, having retired two years earlier, he and Grandma Stone had moved from Ohio to Florida and were on a sightseeing trip to Key West. Apparently he wanted an inexpensive souvenir that has now been handed down through the family.

When I see this memorable bookmark in one of my current reading books, I wonder about his personal story. Where was Granddaddy born? Who were his parents? How did he and his wife of sixty-five years meet? Did he have any hobbies or serve in the military? What's his favorite food? What was his life like in the early part of the twentieth century? How did he happen to become a Christian? What words of wisdom would he have wanted to pass on to his children, grandchildren, and great grandchildren?

Now, a couple of generations later, all twelve of my grandchildren call me Granddaddy, and they are teaching their children to address me with that truly honorable title. Yet they really do not know who I am inside— my personal struggles, my family background, my work and educational experiences. They don't know how I met my wife, Mary Lou, whom they affectionately called Nana. They might be surprised at some of the marriage values we cultivated that kept us loving each other for fifty-eight years. Every family goes through tragedy, disappointment, and failure. I wonder how my grandchildren will handle their setbacks in life as well as their successes, and whether they could gain anything by knowing something of mine. I was baptized in the Roman Catholic Church as an infant, but I retired at age sixty-five after many years of service in the United Methodist ministry. They don't know how all that came about. The questions raised are almost endless.

Letters to Christopher is the title I chose as a vehicle to convey my comings and goings through the years. Christopher, my first great grandchild's name, actually represents all of my children and grandchildren, those living and those yet to be born. My creative imagination pictures younger family members becoming genuinely curious and interested enough to shake our family tree and see what might fall out. Also, those who read this book might want to consider bringing their spiritual journey into focus through the lens of their own family stories. *Letters to Christopher* could serve as a springboard for telling, sharing, and preserving your family's history. Ponder this invitation from noted author David Baldacci.

> Once we reach adulthood, most of us assume we know all there is to know about our parents and other family members. However, if you take the time to ask questions and actually listen to the answers, you may find there is still

much to learn about people close to you. Oral histories are a dying art, which is sad indeed for they show appropriate respect for the lives and experiences of those who have come before. And, just as important, they document those remembrances, for once those lives are over, that personal knowledge is lost forever. Unfortunately, we live in a time now where everyone seems to be solely looking ahead, as though we deem nothing in the past worthy of our attention. The future is always fresh and exciting, and it has a pull on us that times past simply can never muster. Yet it may well be that our greater wealth as human beings can be discovered by simply looking behind us.[1]

Conversation and storytelling guides are included in the appendices for family gatherings, for small group sharing, and for personal reflections. Because a good book is good company, I hope all who read about my legacy bookmark find themselves in good company.

James K. Wagner

Preface
Unique and Unusual Correspondence

Christopher,

You are probably surprised to get a letter from me in response to your e-mail inquiry. I could have answered you with a reply e-mail, but then I figured you might like to have a hard copy, something to read and think about when you are so inclined. Be assured I am somewhat familiar with social media. Smart phones, cell phones, iPads, laptops, tablets, Twitter, Facebook, texting, Instagram, and e-mails are okay, but they're not the vehicles I want to use in responding to your good questions. Brief messages have their place and purpose. However, the subjects and issues you are raising deserve thoughtful, considered, prayerful responses. It would be better if we could talk face-to-face, but geography prohibits that. Your e-mails and my letters will have to do for now.

Granddaddy

Okay, Granddaddy. Keep those hard copies coming. Let's begin with some personal questions. My mom said you were raised in the Catholic Church. So were your parents Catholic or what? What was your family like? Tell me about your growing up years. What happened that caused you to become a United Methodist minister?

Christopher

Letter 1
Calling the Unqualified

No eye has seen, nor ear heard, nor the human heart conceived,
what God has prepared for those who love him.
—1 Corinthians 2:9 (NRSV)

Christopher,

Someone once said, "God calls the unqualified and then equips those who are called." My beginnings and early years certainly spell "unqualified to pursue a career in Christian ministry." Because you asked about my family background, I will start there.

Piqua, Ohio, a small town along the banks of the Miami River, was a good place to be born on August 24, 1934. Both my mother's parents and my father's parents were what we would call today working poor. They lived from paycheck to paycheck, practiced a frugal lifestyle, and believed that family, country, and church were a trinity to be honored.

However, not all was well in these two clans. My father, Kenneth Franke, and his family were Roman Catholic. My mother, Lillian, and her family were members of the United Brethren in Christ Church. I never heard how they met or how long they dated, but they got married in St. Boniface Roman Catholic Church. Mother never converted to the Catholic faith, however she did sign a document in the presence of a priest stating that if any children were born in the marriage, they would be baptized in the Catholic Church and sent to Catholic parochial school. Our mother kept her promise. Even though the marriage did not last, my younger brother, Lynn, and I were both baptized at St. Boniface and sent to the Catholic elementary school next door to the church.

In the early 1940s, my parents got divorced, just as World War II was getting underway. Mother had custody of her two sons, and she had to work hard to support us. At one point we would have become homeless, except her parents, Grandma and Granddaddy Stone, took us in for several months until Mother could generate some income.

When I was in the fifth grade, my father died. I remember attending his funeral and being told his death was from liver disease brought on by excessive alcohol consumption. I was only about five or six when he moved out of our life, and so I have very few memories of my biological father.

During those war years, Grandma Stone watched Lynn, and Grandma Franke took care of me while Mother worked long hours in what they called a defense plant. Walking sixteen long blocks, I would go to mass on Sundays with Grandma Franke, who was the only woman in her family of seven brothers. She often shared with me stories of her hardships and difficult times growing up. More than once, Grandma Franke told me that when she died, she was going straight to heaven because she already had her purgatory on earth. We never had discussions or arguments about these two Christian traditions in our family. We simply accepted that which could not be changed, loved one another, and took each day as it came along.

Both grandmothers were excellent cooks, fixing wonderful meals on tight budgets. One day when someone complimented her after eating a piece of her cake, I recall Grandma Stone responding, "I'll tell you secret. I never had a cake fall in the oven. Every time I put one in to bake, I say, 'This cake's for you, Jesus.'" I regret not getting her recipe for chicken potpie, my very favorite meal in her dining room.

We did not have kindergarten back in those days, and so Grandma Stone set up a chalkboard in her kitchen and taught me the alphabet, simple math, and some basic spelling at age five. I was well prepared to enter first grade. I must credit Grandma Franke with teaching me to play euchre, a German card game. Since then, euchre has been an inexpensive source of fun and enjoyment for our children and grandchildren. Her specialty in the kitchen was roast pork, sauerkraut, and mashed potatoes, with homemade bread still warm from the oven.

I cringe when parents tell me that they do not take their children to church because they want them to be open-minded and free to make their own religious choices later in life. I wonder if these same parents would deny their daughters and sons an elementary education so that when they were older, they could decide if they really wanted to go to school. A foundation in Christian education is a vital necessity for youth to explore spirituality and begin to know the reality of God. Here, I want to express a high degree of appreciation to the Roman Catholic Church for baptizing, confirming, and receiving me into membership. I sang in a children's choir and served as an altar boy, assisting the priest at mass in Latin. My first Holy Communion at age seven was a deeply spiritual experience. I well recall one afternoon after school in the sixth grade, knocking on the door of the parish priest and asking to see him.

Priest: Well, Jim, what brings you here today?

Me: Father, I have something I want you to know.

Priest: And what might that be?

Me: I think God wants me to be a priest.

Priest: Well, Jim, that's interesting. Tell you what. After you graduate from high school, if you still want to become a priest, come back, and we'll talk about your next steps.

Deflated, I walked home carrying what I would describe as a spiritual flat tire. Reflecting on that grade school incident, I do believe I was experiencing God's genuine call to the unqualified.

Yet a seed was planted in my soul to be germinated, grown, and harvested several years later. My teachers in elementary school, the Catholic sisters, gave me a lifelong appreciation for the sacraments, worship, hymns, the Ten Commandments, and the therapeutic values of confession and forgiveness. When temptations arose, I was taught to call on Jesus for spiritual help to do the right thing and live with a clear conscience.

Another early memory centers around YMCA summer camp, where I was introduced to the YMCA triangle logo depicting the connection between spiritual, physical, and mental health. It made a lasting impression, although I never heard about this holistic concept in church.

Around 1943, Mother met Harold Wagner. They both worked at the

Lear Aviation Company, began dating, and had a brief courtship until Harold was drafted into the army. Then one Friday after work, Mother boarded a train bound for the army base where Harold was stationed, and they got married. My brother and I were not told about this new relationship until Mother returned. Surprise, surprise! We were too young to understand what that could mean for us and for our future.

After World War II ended in 1945, Harold came back to Piqua, having served in Europe with the famed General George Patton. Soon Mother announced that the four of us were moving north to Celina, Ohio, Harold's boyhood home. As Lynn and I became more acquainted with Harold, he seemed okay, and Mother was happy. She also informed us that Harold wanted to adopt us so that we could be a family with the same last name. She was in favor of that, but was it okay with us? "I guess it's all right," we mumbled. A short time later, we were all seated in front of a judge in a Miami County courthouse. He asked us some questions about what life was like in our home. Were there any problems? Did we have anything to say about the pending adoption? No questions, no problems. Adoption granted. Actually, the only problem I encountered was with my good buddies, who did not care for the Wagner name and insisted on calling me Jimmy Franke. Eventually they got on board, as did all of our relatives.

That summer we migrated north to Celina, Ohio, in Mercer County on the western edge of Grand Lake St. Marys, a large body of water dug to be a feeder for the Miami and Erie Canals in 1845. Harold, along with help from our family on weekends and holidays, built us a modest concrete block house across the street from his parents' home. That fall, Lynn and I enrolled in public schools, he in the third grade and I in the seventh grade. My first day in junior high school turned out to be a daunting challenge. With no preparation, I was upgraded from a small Catholic grade school—where we had been taught all day in one-half of the room while the other half was occupied by another grade level—to being assigned a homeroom, with bells going off every hour or so signaling time to go to another room for another subject by another teacher. How confusing!

Throughout junior high and high school, I went to mass every week. My brother and parents mostly stayed home on Sunday mornings, not following through on their verbal commitment to attend a Presbyterian church.

It was during those teenage years that I went to work for Bob Cole, an energetic, likable jack-of-all-trades and entrepreneur. He owned and operated a small meat market and grocery store, as well as a drive-in restaurant. In the eighth grade, I became his short-order cook. He also taught me how to cut meat and wait on customers. Back in the 1950s, drive-in restaurants were the McDonald's of the day, relying on teenage carhops. Cole's Drive-in was known all over town as the place to get a summer job. He employed hundreds of teenagers in the years he operated his popular drive-in, not only giving young people an opportunity to earn money but also instilling in them the discipline of showing up on time and giving the employer 100 percent. I got my driver's license at age sixteen and had enough money in the bank to buy my first preowned car, a 1941 Chevy Coupe. Working for Bob Cole was demanding yet rewarding. He kept giving me more responsibilities, such as driving his cargo truck to pick up fresh meat at the slaughterhouse some fifty miles away and learning how to do simple electrical, plumbing, and carpentry projects.

Bob Cole became the exemplary male role model that I did not have at home. Bob and his wife, Hazel, had four children and a harmonious marriage, and they were well respected in the community. His ethical business practices and belief in the potential of teenagers earned him my lifelong loyalty. For instance, Bob Cole's positive attitude toward his customers made a lasting impression. In one sentence, it was, "The customer is not always right, but we always treat each customer right." With that attitude, he generated goodwill and good business. Bob's enterprises expanded to include a motel and trailer park next to his drive-in. Several other restaurants in town relied on him to provide them with fresh meat and poultry. In later years, he became known for his indoor flea market and antique store.

During my last year in high school, the question asked of all seniors surfaced: "What are your plans after you graduate?" Bob Cole discussed the possibility of my staying on full time with him, perhaps going into motel and restaurant management. My parents liked that idea. I was quite comfortable living in Celina and spending time with school friends. But then something unforeseen happened. In the spring of that senior year, my English teacher, Miss Winklejohn, kept me after school for a conversation that turned out to be a lecture. "What's this I hear about you not going on to college?"

I told her, "I have not given that much thought and will probably get a good job in Celina." For the next half hour, Miss Winklejohn let me know how disappointed she was to hear me say that, and she listed several reasons for me to get out of Celina, get a higher education, and pursue a professional career. I thanked her for her concern but informed her that our family was not much on college education.

Not long after that, our high school sponsored a career day, which meant that representatives of the US military, several corporations, and about half a dozen Ohio colleges came for student inquiries and interviews, distributing their information. Almost the entire senior class showed up.

The Otterbein College table caught my attention. The only person in our family who had ever gone to college was my mother's brother, James Stone, who'd gone to Otterbein right after the war, when the government encouraged veterans with financial aid (called the GI Bill). I did not know much about Otterbein, except James had gone there, had graduated, and was teaching history in a high school near Akron, Ohio; he later became the principal. I casually spoke with Professor James Ray at the Otterbein display, telling him about my uncle.

He said, "Would you like to visit our campus sometime? I would be happy to meet you there and give you a personal tour. Tell me some of your interests, Jim. What kinds of activities are you involved in here in Celina High? Have you thought about what you might do after graduation?" As Dr. Ray quietly and calmly engaged me in conversation, I found myself becoming somewhat curious and left him with a possibility of coming for a campus visit.

Well, Christopher, now you know something about my growing-up years. Hope you don't mind all the details. I tend to get a bit wordy. What were some of those other questions you had?

Granddaddy

Letter 2
Qualifying the Unqualified

The church: a fellowship wherein we agree to
differ resolve to love, unite to serve.
—E. Stanley Jones

Christopher,

From your recent e-mail, it looks as though in my last letter, you especially liked all the references to WWII, something you have only known from movies and history books. Because you asked about the circumstances around my decision to leave the Catholic Church and become a United Methodist minister, let's pick up my story after high school.

With Miss Winklejohn's encouragement, I did contact Dr. James Ray and set a date to visit the Otterbein campus. This professor of English literature gave me an extensive tour, introducing me to several faculty members along the way. What really impressed me were the friendly greetings from all the students we met. When I mentioned that my main extracurricular interest in high school was music (having sung in several choirs, played in the marching band and orchestra, and directed the student pep band at home basketball games), he arranged a meeting with the head of the music department, Dr. Lee Shackson, who explained the basic academic requirements for a music education degree. He suggested I discuss it with my parents and get back to him. He also said I would probably be eligible for some financial assistance, which he called scholarship funds.

Mother was delighted that I had an interest in Otterbein, except there was no money for college. If I went, I would have to work my way all four years. She promised to pray for me every day and cook wonderful meals whenever I could get home. And so it happened that the first week of

September 1952, I arrived at Otterbein College enrolled as a freshman with a major in music education and a minor in the Air Force Reserved Officers Training Corp (AFROTC).

You might be wondering how the air force entered the picture. Simple explanation: the Korean War was in full swing, and nineteen-year-olds were being drafted into the US Army. To get a draft deferral and stay in college, AFROTC was the logical choice for me and about half of the freshman class at Otterbein, although this meant a three-year commitment with active duty in the air force after graduation.

Founded in 1847, Otterbein College is named after Phillip William Otterbein (1726–1813), a German Reformed Church missionary who came to the United States to start new congregations. This liberal arts college located in Westerville, a northern suburb of Columbus, Ohio, claimed an enrollment slightly more than six hundred in the 1950s. Now called Otterbein University with an enrollment approaching four thousand, the school continues to uphold the highest academic standards, along with Christian values, genuine friendliness, a hospitable environment, and a welcoming campus.

Soon a new person entered my life and gave me another reason to enjoy Otterbein. In those days, all students were required to attend chapel services four mornings a week. We had to sit alphabetically for the attendance takers. Those with last names starting with *W* sat close to the *S* students. There I met Mary Lou Stine, a freshman also majoring in music education. She was a charming and beautiful young woman. We had many classes together, became well acquainted, and started to date. By the end of that first school year, we were a couple.

However, Mary Lou's parents were not pleased when they discovered their daughter, an only child, was dating a Catholic boy. Her father was a minister in the Evangelical United Brethren Church (EUB) in Dayton, Ohio. Nevertheless, we continued to see each other on a regular basis throughout our time at Otterbein. Getting married was discussed, but it was problematic given our religious backgrounds. We both agreed that if we did get married and should have children, neither of us wanted competing church loyalties. Consequently, Mary Lou counseled with my priest, and I met with the campus minister.

This uncertainty about our future relationship led us to exploring the

Christian faith in various traditions. For several months, we intentionally attended neutral churches such as Lutheran, Presbyterian, and Episcopal. Nothing seemed to open a possible path, until I happened to read a book by Roland Bainton, *Here I Stand,* a biography of the sixteenth-century church reformer Martin Luther.[2]

What a revelation to discover that Catholics and non-Catholics follow the same Jesus, read the same Bible, and promote prayer, faith, and responsible moral living. This book prompted me to begin reading the Bible and focus on the Gospels, where I discovered that Jesus Christ, the head and Lord of the Church, never prescribed an organizational structure. He simply and profoundly said, "Follow me." Throughout the four Gospels, Jesus presented this invitation to many people who are not named, as well as to his twelve apostles who are named. I find it quite interesting that in the final conversation Jesus had with Peter, as recorded in John 21:19 NRSV, he said the very same words as when he first recruited Peter: "Follow me" (Mark 1:16–20 NRSV). This gracious invitation continues to this day to everyone who, for whatever reason, is attracted to Jesus. I concluded that no one church, congregation, or denomination has a monopoly on spiritual issues and that there are multiple and diverse ways to follow Jesus.

Christopher, all this may seem a bit strange that I would even think this way, but you have to remember I was indoctrinated in grade school to believe that the Roman Catholic Church was the true Church, having been started when Jesus said to Peter, "On this rock [Peter] I will build my church ... I'll give you the keys of the kingdom of heaven" (Matthew 16:18–19 NRSV).

We were even told to stay off the sidewalk in front of the Lutheran church across the street from our Catholic parochial school. Why? Because Martin Luther, a Catholic priest, disobeyed the pope, caused many problems, and started the Lutheran Church. Actually, history testifies that initially Martin Luther had no intention of creating a new church. Primarily in 1516, he was trying to change certain practices within the Catholic Church. When that proved to be impossible, the followers of this German reformer organized the Lutheran Church, and the Protestant Reformation got underway throughout Europe. Since those tumultuous times, the Catholic Church has experienced several reforms.

Thankfully, today Catholics and Protestants engage in interfaith dialogue, acknowledging Jesus Christ as Lord and Savior. We do not insist on every Christian having the same theology and church policies. We look for those areas of Christian faith where we can work together for the good of world. In the late 1960s when the pope encouraged cooperation with non-Catholics rather than separation, I was invited to preach in an ecumenical service in a Catholic Church. We even sang Martin Luther's great hymn "A Mighty Fortress Is Our God," an amazing grace moment to not forget.

Back to the courtship of Jim and Mary Lou. As we were entering our senior year at Otterbein, I decided to experiment being a Protestant. I stopped going to mass and went to church with Mary Lou at the First Evangelical United Brethren Church in Westerville. We worshiped together, sang in the choir, and liked the senior pastor, Dr. M. J. Miller. This arrangement proved to be workable, comfortable, and spiritually satisfying.

In the spring before graduation, I received a memo from the college treasurer informing me that even though I was meeting all academic requirements, I would not receive a diploma until all bills were paid. Specifically, I owed several hundred dollars for tuition fees. I quickly liquidated all my assets to raise the needed funds, selling my tuxedo, string bass, baseball glove, books, and anything slightly valuable. I depleted my meager bank account. Debt paid in full.

Next, I asked Mary Lou for her hand in marriage. She said, "Of course, but you need to discuss it with my father." Rev. Lorin Stine gave us his blessing. Five days after graduation from Otterbein College, Mary Lou's father married us at the Fairview EUB Church in Dayton, Ohio, on June 9, 1956. A few weeks later, I joined that church, and we lived in Dayton until I was called to active duty with the United States Air Force in December.

Now, it so happened that six blocks from Fairview Church was the campus of United Theological Seminary (UTS). Even though I seemed to be okay with my new church relationship, I still had questions about interpreting the Bible, the theology of Christian faith, and the life, death, and resurrection of Jesus. Late in August, I met with Dr. Bruce Behney, dean of the seminary. I explained my background and wondered if I could enroll in the fall term—not with the intention of completing a degree or going into ministry, but rather to ask questions, seek answers, and be a more informed Christian. His response was, "Come on in." I did complete that quarter at UTS and then reported for duty at Lackland Air Force Base, San Antonio,

Texas, about two weeks before Christmas. God was beginning to qualify the unqualified with my intrepid entry into the seminary community.

In January 1957, Mary Lou joined me at Hondo Air Base, not far from San Antonio. While we were stationed there, our first child, Lauren Jo, was born on Easter Sunday. After completing basic pilot training, my next move was to Laredo Air Force Base, Laredo, Texas (located across the Rio Grande River from Mexico). Soon the air force determined that I was not a competent candidate for flying jet aircraft. Reassignment came to Richards-Gebaur AFB near Kansas City, Missouri, with my primary responsibilities as personnel officer and adjutant. The Kansas City area felt more like Ohio with abundant trees, green grass, and gardens. We were glad to leave the desert area of South Texas.

Finding a new church home was settled the first Sunday we visited Calvary EUB Church. We never forgot the sincere welcome by the pastor and the congregation. One family invited us home with them for dinner. As I recall, they had one scrawny baked chicken, along with a few side dishes and a meager dessert that fed eight of us that day. However, we did not go home hungry, and we knew we had experienced genuine Christian hospitality. Not long after that, I accepted the role of choir director with our new church family.

Everything seemed to be going well until tragic word came to us in October 1958 that Mary Lou's father and two other EUB pastors were killed in a head-on auto accident. They had been coming back to Ohio from a church conference in Harrisburg, Pennsylvania. We immediately packed suitcases and loaded the car (a small Volkswagen Beetle), and the three of us drove to Dayton to be with Freda, Mary Lou's mother. I well remember standing in the long receiving line with them as grief-stricken parishioners and friends came by, attempting to offer a helpful word. One of them said, "Now, Freda, even though we don't understand why this happened, we know it was God's will. Things have a way of working out."

My normally calm and collected mother-in-law responded on a loud voice, "Do not say that. It was not God's will for the horrible accident to happen. It was driver error. End of discussion." That theological lesson deeply registered with me. The next day we gathered in the church for the funeral. Several EUB ministers presided. As I sat there trying to absorb the music, scriptures, and heart-felt tributes, a calming presence seemed to come over me and no doubt others in that sanctuary. Could this be the "peace of God which surpasses all understanding" (Philippians 4:7 NRSV)?

In June 1959, Mary Lou gave birth to our second daughter, Kerril Elizabeth, in Belton, Missouri. During my years in the air force, we were active in the base chapels and in community churches. We accepted the nomadic insecurities of military life with positive attitudes. As a wise person once said, "Attitude, not aptitude, determines one's altitude." Toward the end of my air force obligation, this question called for attention and decision: "What's next?" Three options emerged: (1) stay in the air force with a long-term career, (2) find a high school teaching job, (3) return to Ohio and enroll in the seminary.

As Mary Lou and I prayed, discussed, and shared this decision-making dilemma with close friends, option three surfaced for serious consideration. Through it all, I continued to experience a gentle nudge by the Holy Spirit to accept God's call in my life. This led me to contact Dr. Walter Roberts, the president of UTS, to explore the possibility of coming back to Dayton in September, provided the air force would give me two months early out; my three-year contract was over in December 1959. Answers to our prayers came when the air force agreed and changed my status from active duty to inactive reserve. UTS accepted my application, and we moved in with Mary Lou's mother in Dayton, ten blocks from the seminary campus. That living arrangement proved to be a win-win situation. Mary Lou got a position teaching elementary school music in Dayton, I was hired as a part-time minister of music and youth director at the Oak Street EUB Church, and our two young daughters loved living with their Grammy. The Fairview EUB Church formally endorsed and recommended me as a candidate for full-time ministry. Consequently, I was ordained with ministerial credentials in the Evangelical United Brethren Church following graduation with a master's of divinity degree from UTS in June 1962.

So, Christopher, looking back on all that Mary Lou and I experienced in our first six years of marriage, I am convinced that God was quietly preparing us for an unpredictable yet certain future. Having changed addresses five times in the air force, we were ready to accept the itinerant system of moving ministers in the EUB Church, going where the bishop appointed us. That's about it for now. I look forward to your next e-mail.

Granddaddy

Letter 3
Equipping the Called

To equip God's people for the work of serving
and building up the body of Christ.
—Ephesians 4:12 (CEB)

Christopher,

Now you have the answer to why I left the Catholic Church, and that leads to your next question: What happened to the Evangelical United Brethren Church connection, considering I am presently serving in the United Methodist Church?

Upon graduating from the seminary, I was offered a full-time position back in Westerville with the First Evangelical United Brethren Church as an associate pastor. After much prayer and discussion with Mary Lou and several good friends, I accepted the offer. It meant I would be working with Senior Pastor Dr. M. J. Miller, a seasoned mentor. Plus, the church was next to the Otterbein College campus, a reminder of our formative student days. Although I remained convinced that God's call was authentic, I was still uncertain whether I had the necessary skills and abilities for a career in Christian ministry. At that time, I had little desire to preach, but I readily agreed to take responsibilities for Christian education and music ministry.

Looking back on those early days, I began to understand what Jesus had in mind when he said to his potential disciples, "Follow me." Just like those first followers, we too are attracted to Jesus, though we may hesitate to say yes because of our personal limitations and inadequacies. On the other hand, Jesus knows our potential and proceeds to equip those who say yes to his gracious invitation. This equipping process seems to be endless, yet it is experienced exactly as needed for the task at hand. I compare Jesus's ongoing efforts in qualifying those he calls as continuing education, similar at times to what is known as on-the-job training (OJT). I have also come to believe that in God's economy, nothing is wasted and tends to get recycled. This includes part-time jobs and what may appear at the moment to be insignificant accomplishments. No one likes to fail; everyone wants to succeed. Yet if we do not learn anything from our failures, we are destined to repeat them and enjoy limited successes. As I continued to reflect on where I had been so far in life, I began to make a list of all the paying jobs I'd held from grade school through my seminary training years:

> delivering newspapers, selling ice cream from bicycle carts, stocking shelves in a grocery store, washing cars, setting pins in a bowling alley, short-order cooking, making ice cream, peeling and processing potatoes for french fries, cutting meat, clerking in a grocery store, working on an assembly line in a clothing factory, delivering flowers, playing string bass in a square dance group and in a jazz band, being custodian for a restaurant and a dentist office, washing dishes and serving food, landscaping, building maintenance, managing a fraternity boarding club, ministering to youth, and directing choirs

Repeatedly, I have been able to incorporate these early employment experiences in later life situations. What often felt like a waste of time turned out to be beneficial. These temporary jobs not only instilled a better understanding of that line of work, but they also gave me an appreciation for all who have very few employment options and who have to work full time in those areas where I was a temporary employee.

We enjoyed living in Westerville, a good place to raise our two daughters, and things seemed to be going well at the church. However, the 1960s were tumultuous times for our country, dealing with Civil Rights issues, the Vietnam War, and then the assassination of President John Kennedy in November 1963. These and other challenges deeply impacted college campuses throughout the United States. The invasion of the Beatles from England upturned American youth culture, and someone even suggested that perhaps it would be okay to have music in the church sanctuary accompanied by drums and guitars.

Associate pastors are usually asked to preach on the Sundays when the senior pastor is absent. Translated: I was the preacher at the First EUB Church three or four times a year—an opportunity that began to appeal to me as more pulpit time was afforded. I still entered fully in my responsibilities with Christian education and music ministries, but I began to raise questions. Is this where God wants me to be? Should I consider being a pastor? Is my family open to moving to another church? Because Mary Lou was willing to consider a different assignment, I discussed this with Dr. Miller and wrote a letter to our bishop requesting an appointment as pastor. If God wanted me to be a pastor, I was convinced that the equipping process would continue.

Next came a phone call from Dr. William Messmer, the superintendent of the EUB churches in the southwestern part of Ohio. As I recall, it was in April 1964. He informed me that he knew of three churches that would soon be changing pastors: Englewood Church and Southern Hills Church in the Dayton suburbs, and a church in Cincinnati. Dr. Messmer suggested that I take a drive with my family to look over the neighborhoods where these churches were located. However, he cautioned not to enter the church buildings or discuss this with anyone except my wife. Back in those days, the moving of pastors was not made public until the bishop read the list of church appointments at the annual meeting of the EUB Conference in the summer.

On a rainy Saturday, we drove around these three churches. We reviewed their statistics in the EUB journal, discussed them, prayed about them, and then contacted Dr. Messmer with our personal preferences. In order, they were the Cincinnati church, the Englewood Church, and the Southern Hills Church. Soon after that, we were informed of the bishop's decision: we were going to Southern Hills. For a moment I thought I was back in the military, where the very same thing had happened to me: multiple air force base openings would be posted, but I rarely got my first choice.

Mary Lou and I, along with our two young daughters, arrived at the Southern Hills Church and parsonage in late June 1964. The congregation and lay leaders were more than gracious in their welcoming introductions. We soon came to believe this was where God had intended us to be.

Challenge number one was getting to know the people by making house calls and setting up small group meetings of members by neighborhoods.

Challenge number two was that the church membership roll had not been audited for several years. What was billed as a church of 400 members turned out to be around 250. My preaching and teaching ministry were launched and well received. Pastoral calls in hospital and nursing homes, along with counseling and daily contacts with parishioners, reinforced and blessed this budding pastor. Mary Lou organized a children's choir, and our daughters conveniently walked two blocks to their elementary school.

Challenge number three, was the one thing lacking: no nursery on Sunday mornings for babies. Why? Because there were no babies in the congregation, until Mary Lou gave birth to our son, James Tobin, whom we called Toby, in February 1965. That proved to be something of a catalyst and a magnet, attracting younger couples who brought their babies. Soon we had to provide a church nursery for worship and various gatherings. Taken to church from the time he was a week old, Toby was practically raised by our caring congregation.

One family story that we continue to tell happened when Toby was about four years old. Our church hosted the monthly meetings of the community's senior citizens club. That meant that Toby's older buddy Charlie would stop by the parsonage to see if our son could tag along with him. One time he informed his mother, "Bye. I'm going with Charlie to the senior sins."

Christopher, your answer to the change in my denomination affiliation came about during our time at Southern Hills. For many years, the Evangelical United Brethren Church and the Methodist Church had been seriously discussing this possibility of a merger. It almost happened early in the nineteenth century in Baltimore. Similar theology, parallel church organizations, and common mission goals characterized both sides. However, the Methodists ministered primarily to English-speaking settlers, whereas the EUB planted German-speaking churches. Finally, when ongoing merger talks came to fruition in 1968, the church I served was renamed the Southern Hills United Methodist Church, and I became a United Methodist minister.

The year 1968 also proved to be a milestone year when I enrolled at Earlham School of Religion in Richmond, Indiana, to take a course in religious journalism, taught by the well-known Quaker author and philosopher Dr. Elton Trueblood. This was an excellent decision. Even though I did learn much about writing for publication, better still were the insights gained from Dr. Trueblood's gifted understanding of church renewal and the role of minister and laity. He taught our class that the primary role of the pastor was to encourage, motivate, train, and enable Christians to do ministry, not to do their ministry for them. The bottom line was not, "What do I want the Church to be and to do?" Rather it was, "What does Jesus Christ, the foundation and Lord of the church, want His Church to be and to do?" This refreshing awareness caused me to rethink my role and leadership style as pastor.

Trying to be the answer man and be available twenty-four seven to fix everyone's problems was not only wearisome but a one-way ticket to professional burnout. Then I discovered this liberating word from Jesus in the very last sentence in the Gospel of Matthew 28:20 (NRSV). "And remember, I am with you always, to the end of the age." This saving word is for clergy and laity alike. At times we may feel like spiritual orphans, but Jesus never leaves us. He keeps his promise to all generations of followers: "I will not leave you orphaned. The Holy Spirit, whom the Father will send in my name, will teach you everything, and remind you of all that I have said to you. Do not let your hearts be troubled, neither let them be afraid. My peace I give to you" (John 14:18–27 NRSV).

During this pastorate, an amazing, ministry-changing moment came as I was casually reading a newspaper article in Greenville, Ohio's *Daily Advocate*. This headline on April 10, 1969, arrested my attention.

Annual Spiritual Healing Mission to Be Held at Presbyterian Church in Middletown

My interest was further piqued as I discovered that this was their second annual Spiritual Healing Mission, slated for April 20–22, and the guest minister and speaker was the Reverend Dr. Alfred W. Price, from the historic St. Stephen's Episcopal Church in Philadelphia. Dr. Price had been conducting healing services for several years. His goal was to help restore Christian healing ministry to its proper place in present-day churches.

Nothing that I read in that article made any sense to me. In seminary we did not hear or learn about healing ministry. Yet here were mainline churches engaging in what many labeled as controversial activity, mostly relegated to independent churches and TV evangelists. Because my curiosity would not go away, I decided to drive to Middletown, a short distance from Dayton, to see what this was all about. For the Sunday evening healing service, I situated myself in the balcony as an observer, not a participant.

As I recall, there were well over two hundred in the congregations that night. The order of service was not complicated, with hymns, scripture readings, and a sermon by Dr. Price. Toward the end of his message, he gave an invitation to all who would like personal prayer for themselves or for another person to come forward to the communion railing for anointing with oil and laying on hands, as instructed in the Epistle of James 5:13–16. The organist began to play softly, and I assumed that Dr. Price would do the one-on-one prayers. Not so! He sat down, and there emerged five or six prayer teams, with two persons on each team. Obviously this was a combination of laity and clergy offering the prayers for healing. I was impressed with the peacefulness and quiet calm pervading the sanctuary as dozens of worshipers made their way forward, some in wheelchairs. Then it came to me that if I really wanted to know what this was all about, I needed to go forward, walk down that long aisle, and present myself for personal prayer. So I did.

A team of two women beckoned me to their prayer station. I knelt. One asked if I had a personal request. I said, "No, just pray with me." I do not remember the words of that prayer, but I well recall that it was brief and that the anointing with oil in the form of a cross on my forehead, along with their gentle physical touch, was like receiving the bread and the cup in Holy Communion. I arose, thanked them, and made my way back to my seat. Instantly I became convinced that this was authentic, Christ-centered ministry that I was not offering my congregation at the Southern Hills Church. I took seriously teaching and preaching, but not healing, even though the Gospels clearly record Jesus instructing his disciples to continue his threefold ministry (see Matthew 4:23; Matthew 9:35; John 14:12–14; Matthew 28:18–20 NRSV).

Upon arriving home, I shared this amazing epiphany with Mary Lou. After engaging a babysitter for our children, we returned the next evening for another exposure and more participation in that Presbyterian-hosted, healing mission. From that moment on, Mary Lou and I were a team in developing and offering various formats for intentional healing ministries.[3]

Was it purely coincidental that I just happened to read that newspaper article? Or was it a God-incident? Could it be that surprisingly, helpful coincidences are initiated by God, who chooses to remain anonymous? Or as a friend of mine puts it, "When I pray, coincidences happen, and when I don't, they don't." When I discovered a half dozen or so parishioners who had a similar interest in healing ministry at the Southern Hills Church, we began timidly yet boldly offering once-a-month Sunday afternoon Holy Communion and healing services. Calling this an experimental ministry with built-in evaluations, we were able to overcome the skeptics, who stayed away but allowed us to proceed. After six months, with attendance averaging twelve to twenty, the Church Administrative Board gave us permission to continue the experiment because it was proving to be a blessing for those who participated.

By this time, I had no doubt that all of this was further evidence of the equipping process intended for me to become more qualified and effective as a Christian minister.

Christopher, I'm sure all of this raises more questions. Let's keep in touch.

Granddaddy

Letter 4
Hardwired to God

The most important dimension to health is spiritual.
—David Hilton, MD

Christopher,

You seem to be a bit uncomfortable and have concerns about my decision to conduct healing services. Perhaps I need to explain in more detail.

Let's begin with prayer, because prayer ministry is healing ministry. Not long ago, I happened to see a TV interview with James W. Miller, an author and pastor in Los Angeles, who claims that everyone is hard-wired to God. His credible theory is that embedded within the DNA of all human beings is a yearning desire to communicate with our creator.[4]

> God created humanity in God's own image, in the divine image God created male and female. (Genesis 1:27 CEB)

I affirm this observation by Dr. Wayne Dyer, author and motivational speaker: "We are not human beings having a spiritual experience. We are spiritual beings having a human experience."

Furthermore, because I am created in God's image, when my body stops functioning, I shall continue to exist. The apostle Paul referred to his body as a tent in which he lived on earth until he went on to the next realm of existence. (See 2 Corinthians 5:1.) The question is not, "Do I want to be a spiritual person?" Rather it is, "Because I am a spiritual person, whose spirit or what spirit do I choose to follow?" Prayer is the foundational spiritual experience for everyone.

Consider these numerous attributes of prayer.

- I am the God-given craving bred into every human heart.
- I am the newborn's first breath and the dying one's last gasp.
- I am the soul's sincere desire, uttered or unexpressed.
- I am simple enough for small children to understand, yet profound enough to confound the wisest of the wise.
- I am not learned in a classroom, but I am taught through all of life's experiences.
- I am the subject of untold numbers of books, yet as fresh, as radiant, as inviting as the morning sun.
- I am the communication link with the holy one called God.
- I am the primary spiritual therapy.
- I am compassion felt and love expressed.
- I am meditation and contemplation.
- I can be very wordy or totally silent.
- I am at home with those in solitude and with those in a multitude.
- I am the Internet of the soul, reaching outward around the world and reaching inward to all those in my personal world.

I am prayer.

Christopher, there is so much more I could say to you about prayer. Perhaps the Nike slogan says it best: Just do it. And when you pray, try not to do all the talking. Dialogue, not monologue, is the better way. Think of your cell phone. When you call someone, do you not give that person an opportunity to speak? Prayer is a two-way conversation with God. Someone has suggested that if you take only five minutes to pray each day, tell God what's on your heart and mind for two and then simply quiet yourself and listen for three minutes.

Consider this lesson I learned years ago from the Reverend Dr. Morton Kelsey, Episcopal priest and noted author in the field of prayer and healing. Among other things, he emphasized that Jesus's main preaching and teaching theme was the kingdom of God, which he illustrated with dozens of stories called parables. Dr. Kelsey went on to say that the kingdom of God is a spiritual realm and that the Bible consistently deals with the spiritual dimensions of life. To prove his point, he held up an inexpensive paperback copy of the New Testament. He had cut out every word and reference to spiritual phenomena: heaven, hell, angels, God, Holy Spirit, miracles, faith, devil, eternal life, prayer. The result? His NT was reduced to paper lace because some 50 percent had been removed. His point: if you and I do not take seriously the reality of the spiritual realm, we will not understand the Bible and will not have an effective prayer life.

Before I go further, I need to bring you up to date on my next pastoral appointment. In June 1971, we arrived at the parsonage of the Columbia Heights United Methodist Church in Columbus, Ohio, with a membership of nearly six hundred. That September, Toby entered first grade, Kerrie enrolled in junior high, Laurie was a high school freshman, and Mary Lou began teaching music in the Southwestern City School District. Because Jesus ministered to the whole person (body, mind, spirit, and relationships), I continued to look to him for direction, discernment, and leadership in the ongoing process of becoming more qualified. When I announced my interest in healing ministry, several church members came forward with an eagerness to assist. After laying the prerequisite ground work (preaching and teaching based on the healing stories of Jesus, informal small group conversations, prayers for guidance), we received permission from the church's council to begin an experimental healing ministry similar to the Southern Hills Church model, with Sunday afternoon services of Holy Communion and healing prayer once a month. The first Sunday in Advent 1974 became our launch date, with emphases on intercessory prayer, Holy Communion, lay leadership, and participation from neighborhood churches. Typically we had twelve to fifteen in attendance. The local Lutheran pastor asked if he could encourage his parishioners to attend. Of course, all were welcome. Soon he and I agreed to offer weekly Sunday afternoon services, alternating between the two church sanctuaries.

Early in 1975, a brochure came in the mail from United Theological Seminary (UTS) announcing a graduate degree called a doctor of ministry (D.Min.). The focus was on practical applications of Christian ministry. This independent study required three years and a faculty advisor, plus tuition costs. Those who had a master's of divinity and were out of seminary at least five years were eligible to apply. Each class of D.Min. students began with an intensive, five-day orientation in August on campus. After discussing this possibility with my church leaders and getting Mary Lou's blessing, I enrolled with the goal of researching, exploring, and studying holistic healing within the context of a local church.

I knew before I began this intentional journey that I would face resistance. The negative reputation of charlatan faith healers had invaded the church. Several members advised me to stick to preaching and teaching, and to let the hospitals do the healing. A woman in the congregation cautioned, "I think I like the idea, but spiritual healing scares people." A school teacher who recently graduated from college and was active in the church said, "I'll try to keep an open mind, but I warn you, I'm skeptical." Then there was my faculty advisor, who asked me, "Jim, can you use a word other than *healing* in the title of your proposal? That is a loaded word and will raise red flags in the minds of many people." Those remarks reminded me of the late United Methodist Bishop F. Gerald Ensley, who was being criticized for giving so much of his attention to the cause of evangelism. He said, "My doing something is better than your doing nothing." So it is with intentional healing ministry in the church. The rewards are greater than the risks. The blessings are more abundant than the failures. I felt led to legitimize the word *healing* in the church and to offer experiences with the healing Christ.

Christopher, I want to share with you a personal healing story that happened shortly before I was to enter my D.Min. program at UTS. Rarely do I get sick, and it's usually one or two head colds a year. However, five days before the intensive orientation, I developed symptoms of pneumonia or worse. The doctor loaded me with antibiotics and said to get bed rest. My prayer focused on being well enough to drive seventy-five miles to Dayton by the end of the week. But my condition got no better. I knew if I missed the deadline, I would have to wait another year.

Then an amazing thing happened. Mary Lou, in the middle of the night before I was to leave, knelt by my bedside and offered her prayers on my behalf. Immediately we both went to sleep. I woke around 6:00 a.m. breathing normally, head cleared, and feeling refreshed. I got up, showered, dressed, and was halfway packed when Mary Lou woke up.

"What are you doing?"

"I'm getting ready to go to the seminary for the orientation."

"That's ridiculous. You've been very sick. You're too weak."

"I know, but the Lord must have used your prayers last night to strengthen me enough to go. So I'm going."

My research put me in contact with a wide variety of leaders in the art, science, and practice of healing, with Jesus being my primary teacher and role model. While studying the life and ministry of Jesus in the four Gospels (Matthew, Mark, Luke, and John), I quickly became aware that he clearly understood and demonstrated the relationship between physical health, mental health, and spiritual health. The salvation Jesus offered included, but went beyond, spiritual well-being. Because he loved the whole person, his goal was to help each person become whole.[5]

This is quite evident in listing the unhealthiness and brokenness that Jesus dealt with during his public ministry: physical paralysis, blindness, epilepsy, leprosy, dropsy, mental illness, evil spirits, hemorrhaging, muteness, deafness, and death. Further, Jesus never hesitated to counsel people about their personal relationship with God, knowing that resentment, jealousy, anger, and unforgiveness have a negative impact on one's state of health.[6]

Does this mean that churches practicing intentional healing ministry will replace hospitals? No, not at all. God uses medicine, hospitals, various therapies, as well as psychology and psychiatry. However, these resources are insufficient to meet our total health care needs if the spiritual dimension is omitted. When we get sick, we need to locate and combine the best medical care and the best spiritual care. My research has convinced me that each church has the potential to be a primary healing community for these reasons.

The church:

- Engages in whole person ministry (body, mind, spirit, relationships) by offering Christ's ministries of teaching, preaching, and healing.
- Encourages and promotes faith and trust in God.
- Is a laboratory of living prayer.
- Deals with root causes of unhealthiness.
- Becomes an extended family, caring for and loving one another.
- Does personal, one-on-one ministry.
- Works closely with health care professionals.
- Offers spiritual therapies.

- Promotes holistic health practices.
- Is involved in environmental healing of planet Earth.

Jesus operated on the assumption (as does medical research) that disease is not beneficial to humanity. Disease is not to be accepted; rather, it is to be conquered and eliminated. Notice that Jesus never blamed God for a person's illness, and neither did he suggest that sickness is God's way of disciplining wayward people. Jesus never told anyone, "Your sickness is God's will," or, "God made you sick to test your faith."[7]

Francis MacNutt, a Roman Catholic, points out, "Never do we find that Jesus, in the presence of sickness, encourages people to accept their sickness, nor does Jesus give them sermonettes on patience and endurance."[8] He goes on to say that Christians do not need to claim the gift of healing in order to be faithful channels of Christ's healing love. "You don't have to have any special gift. Just love Jesus, pray for persons, and healing happens. That way seems to work as well as the fantastic gifts of famous faith healers."[9]

Obedience to Christ, compassion for people, and faithfulness in following the biblical examples and directions are the necessary ingredients to offer more intentional healing ministries. This passage in the Letter of James gives us insight to healing ministry in New Testament times and provides guidelines for today's churches.

> Are any among you sick? They should call for the elders of the church and have them pray over them, anointing them with oil in the name of the Lord. The prayer of faith will save the sick, and the Lord will raise them up. Anyone who has committed sins will be forgiven. Therefore, confess your sins to one another and pray for one another, so that you may be healed. The prayer of the righteous is powerful and effective. (James 5:14–16 NRSV)

Christopher, let me share a bit more about the significance of prayer throughout all of life and especially in the healing process. My experience is that most everyone prays, but how many pray believing sincerely that prayer makes a positive difference? When you were created, God gave you a precious gift called free will. Because God respects your human freedom and individual choices, it seems to me that God does not override your personal will but stands in the wings, so to speak, patiently waiting for your invitation to get together. Each time you pray, you are giving God permission to act in your life.

One of the best examples of this spiritual truth is recorded in the Book of Revelation 3:20 (NRSV), where Jesus says, "Listen! I am standing at the door knocking; if you hear my voice and open the door, I will come in to be you." Think of the door as the human heart that can only be opened from the inside. Jesus constantly tries to get our attention. He can knock and knock, but he will never force open the door or barge into our personal space. Think of prayer as hearing the knock, opening the door, and offering a genuine invitation for Jesus to come into your life. Think of prayer as being cooperative with God's yearnings. Think of prayer as putting God first. Think of prayer as allowing God to have the driver's seat in your lifelong journey. As someone quipped, "If God is your co-pilot, perhaps you need to change seats."

Being the spiritual beings that we are, prayer is the primary communication mode of the soul—not the least we can do in any situation, but often the most significant thing we can do. God expects us to use all of our experiences, skills, talents, and abilities in any given situation, keeping in mind that prayer is not a substitute for action. Rather, prayer is an action for which there is no substitute. This is bottom line in the healing ministry of the church, intentionally employing prayer therapy in the healing process.

My three-year D.Min. project ended with a joy-filled commencement in the fall of 1978 at UTS. So many learnings, so rich in new experiences, so motivating and encouraging. Among other things, I discovered that the medical community and growing numbers of health care professionals are paying more attention to the spiritual history of patients. I met several hospital chaplains and pastors who are an integral part of the healing team. On two occasions I was on the same program as Dr. Dale A. Matthews, a practicing physician and a credible exponent of the faith factor in the healing process. Based on the research data we now have on hand, he is convinced that your doctor could, from a strictly scientific point of view, recommend religious involvement in a faith community to improve your chances of being able to:

- Stay healthy and avoid life-threatening and disabling diseases like cancer and heart disease
- Recover faster with fewer complications if you do develop a serious illness
- Live longer
- Encounter life-threatening and terminal illnesses with greater peacefulness and less pain
- Avoid mental illnesses like depression or anxiety and cope more effectively with stress
- Steer clear of problems with alcohol, drugs, and tobacco
- Enjoy a happier marriage and family life
- Find a greater sense of meaning and purpose in life[10]

Another example of my encounters with physicians came when I was conducting a seminar on healing prayer for doctors and ministers in Louisville, Kentucky, in a hospital setting. Several minutes into my presentation, a man raised his hand and announced, "I am a Jewish physician, and I just want to say that Christians do not have a monopoly on healing." The room became very quiet at that point.

My response was, "You are absolutely correct, Doctor. Christians do not have a monopoly on healing. No one does. God is limitless in resources and ways of healing human beings. However, Christians follow Christ, who not only demonstrated most effectively healing various kinds of illnesses but also instructed his followers to do likewise. My purpose is to encourage Christians not to overlook or forget that Christ cared for the whole person. He is the Christian's mentor, teacher, and companion in the healing process, with prayer being the primary spiritual therapy."

Perhaps another doctor I met in Cincinnati on a Sunday morning said it best. As the guest minister, I was invited to preach on the subject of the healing ministry of the church. Afterward, an older gentleman came up and rather boldly announced, "Brother Wagner, I am a retired family practice physician. The way I see it, God is our primary physician, and all the doctors on earth are junior partners." Well said!

I thank God for all doctors, nurses, and therapists. Our family is especially grateful for Dr. John H. Genrich, who delivered our first grandchild, Anna, in Colorado Springs. Within hours he determined that Anna's heart was malfunctioning and recommended additional diagnosis and help from a pediatric cardiologist. As they waited for the ambulance to take Anna and her father, Laszlo, to the University of Colorado Medical Center in Denver, some seventy miles away, Grandmother Mary Lou took the doctor aside and said, "Doctor, we are a Christian family, and with your permission we would like to pray with the baby."

His response was, "I think you should. I'm only the helper." They all gathered in the neo-natal unit of that hospital, placed their hands inside the baby's oxygen tent, gently touched her with their fingertips, and offered their prayers.

Laurie, the baby's mother, said, "Anna, Jesus loves you. Mommy and Daddy love you. You are God's child, and God will take care of you. Amen."[11]

Within hours after Anna's arrival at the Denver hospital, the pediatric specialists announced their diagnosis: total anomalous pulmonary venous return, meaning her pulmonary veins were routed incorrectly. Surgery was recommended as soon as possible. When Anna was sixteen days old, she had an open-heart operation to repair her blood flow system. This was an uncommon operation in 1982, and she was given a 50 percent chance of surviving the surgery. Anna not only survived but was strong enough to go home in less than a week. Today, Anna is a healthy young woman, a college graduate, a wife, and a mother of two. We are convinced that Anna received the very best medical treatment available, plus the most effective spiritual therapy called prayer.

Anna's trauma and triumph indelibly stamped these priceless values on the hearts of everyone in her family.

- Prayer is not the last resort, but the first line of defense and the most effective offense God has instilled within all of us.
- Life is too fragile and too precious to be taken casually and for granted.
- People come first; material things are a lesser priority.
- Family love is a special kind of love, not to be taken lightly or neglected, but rather to be nurtured intentionally.
- The local church community is an extended family for each Christian. Therefore, the church family needs to be sensitive to all persons in crises, especially to those who have little or no family.

- We are comforted by God not only for our sakes but also to be a comfort (a source of strength) to others. Christians are blessed to be a blessing!
- God has many delivery systems to channel health, wholeness, and salvation.[12]

Christopher, in closing this rather long letter, I want to share a prayer with you.

> O God, whose grace and mercy flow like an endless river, help each one of us place ourselves in the path of your boundless love and limitless compassion. May we find our spirits renewed, our bodies healed, our minds clearly enlightened, and our hearts overflowing with love, forgiveness, and grace. In Jesus's name, amen.

Letter 5
Moving On

Spiritual formation is the process whereby we grow in
relationship with God and become conformed to Christ.
—Upper Room Ministries

Christopher,

Your positive response to my last letter motivates me to move on to what
happened next. I will not attempt to sugar-coat the life and times of your
Granddaddy—mainly the facts, perhaps with some slight embellishment.
However, because your questing mind wants to learn more about your
family, I will proceed.

After a seven-year pastorate in Columbus, the next relocation for our
family was to Athens, Ohio, where I was appointed to be the senior pastor at
the First United Methodist Church. Athens is the home of Ohio University
(OU), a student body numbering around 15,000 when we arrived in 1978.
At that time, the population of Athens was also close to 15,000, which meant
that from September through May, parking spaces almost disappeared. On
the upside, the provided parsonage was fairly new, had a very functional
floor plan, was quite comfortable, and was above average compared to our
previously occupied church housing.

Laurie was now starting her senior year at Ohio Northern University
(ONU), Kerrie became a sophomore at Otterbein College, and Toby entered
eighth grade. In late June while we were still unpacking, Laurie announced
that she had an engagement ring from Laszlo Bujdoso, also a student at
ONU, and she wanted to get married in August with a formal wedding at the
First UMC. We agreed. With the help of several church members, we put it
all together, which certainly assisted in our getting acquainted quickly with

the congregation. After the wedding, the newlyweds returned to ONU. A couple of years after, that Kerrie received a ring from David Zeuch, also an Otterbein student, and they were married in the Athens Church. After he graduated from Athens High School, Toby enrolled in Otterbein College, where he met his future wife, Leslie Shenkel.

Because our church was next to the OU campus and had a sorority house on each side of the building, we were immersed in student ministry (a plus and a joy). Being a pastor in an academic community proved to be both stimulating and challenging. Based on my research and study of prayer and healing ministry, I had written a manuscript titled *Blessed to Be a Blessing*, with the subtitle "How to have an intentional healing ministry in your church." Not knowing how that ministry focus would be received by the church leaders, I was hesitant to introduce it. However, when it was published by Upper Room Books in Nashville, word got around rather quickly. After reading the book, several church members came to me and asked when I was going to launch this more intentional prayer ministry. With permission of the administrative council, my associate pastor, Reverend David Griebner (a recent graduate from Duke Divinity School) and I started weekly services of Holy Communion and healing at noon on Wednesdays in the church chapel. Even though our membership numbered in the several hundred, attendance on Wednesdays averaged ten to fifteen, and it was not always the same attendees. I learned then and in other church settings that the size of the congregation did not determine the attendance at healing services. People would come when they had a personal need or wanted to pray for loved ones and friends.

The medical doctors, nurses, and therapists in the congregation were quite supportive of this holistic approach to health in body, mind, and spirit, and in relationships. The chairperson of the Pastor/Parish Relations Committee, a retired doctor, was 100 percent in favor. About four years after I arrived at the Athens Church, I was putting on some unneeded weight. With the urging of Mary Lou, I enrolled in the OU physical fitness program designed for community residents. Five days a week, the class met at 6:00 a.m. in the university gym for calisthenics and a jogging and walking routine. I also consulted with a faculty dietician for a personalized eating guide and weight-loss regimen. After about a month into the program, the pounds began to come off.

Then a rather strange thing happened. I woke up one morning and discovered that I had difficulty reading the telephone book. Thinking this was somehow related to my physical fitness efforts, I phoned Dr. Bruce Paxton, an ophthalmologist and member of the church. He and his wife were active in our couples prayer and sharing group.

"Hello, Bruce, this Jim Wagner."

"Hi, Jim. What's up?"

"Bruce, I have a question you can answer. When you lose significant weight, do your eyeballs shrink? I've been on the fitness program for several weeks, and now I can hardly read small print. Is it related?"

"No, it has nothing to do with weight loss. It's part of the aging process. You probably need bifocal eye glasses. Come in, and I'll take a look."

With a prescription in hand, Dr. Paxton referred me to an optometrist for bifocals. What a blessing these eye doctors bring to all whose eyesight needs an assist.

Another blessing came to me after I completed the OU fitness program: Toby and I ran a 10K race together. Here are Mary Lou's own words.

> My mother and I stood in a crowd of cheering people, watching runners cross the finish line of the Athens, Ohio, Indian Summer Six-mile Run. The October sun was hot. The temperatures and humidity that afternoon were unseasonably high. Several runners had passed out as they finished. We were waiting for Jim and Toby, who were running together along the banks of the Hocking River. That Toby, age seventeen, was competing was no surprise, but the fact that Jim, age forty-eight, was running in a race for the first time in his life was truly amazing.

> I became increasingly concerned as runners straggled in. Prayer arose within me. "Lord, help them finish the race. Six months ago, Jim couldn't run six minutes, and now here he is trying to go six miles. Lord, help Toby and Jim encourage each other along the way."

Suddenly, someone from the crowd yelled, "Look, here come Toby and Jim Wagner!" And look I did as Toby grabbed his dad's hand and lifted it in a sign of victory as they crossed the finish line together.[13]

The values I learned from that physical fitness experience continue to guide my exercise and eating habits as I live into my octogenarian years.

Another highlight of my six years at the Athens Church was introducing and teaching the Bethel Bible Series. These short-term courses were designed to address the lack of biblical knowledge, as well as to develop a lifelong interest in Bible study and spiritual formation. With the leadership of my associate pastor David Maze and gifted church members, we were able to expand the numbers of small groups focused on Old and New Testament studies.

Life in Athens and ministry in the First United Methodist Church were an enjoyable combination for me and my family. But then in 1983, a letter came from Reverend Maxie Dunnam, former world editor of the Upper Room in Nashville, inviting me to consider accepting a new position as executive director of the Disciplined Order of Christ (DOC). Based on the fact that I had never heard of the DOC, I wrote back saying I was not intending to leave the pastoral ministry and did not want to work for an organization that might compete with the local church.

Maxie telephoned to say that the DOC was formed in 1945 at the end of World War II with a goal of revitalizing and renewing churches. In fact, one could not be a member of the DOC unless that person was also active in a local church. He asked that I withhold my decision until after I met with Sylvia Zimmer, secretary in the DOC National Office in Ashland, Ohio. Mary Lou and I decided to explore this offer and drove to Ashland for lunch with Sylvia and with Reverend Wilbur Meiser, the treasurer. We were quite impressed with the DOC history and mission statement.

The Disciplined Order of Christ is an ecumenical spiritual movement of persons who are serious about their commitment to Christ and growth in the mind and spirit of Christ.

The founding catalyst of the DOC was the Reverend Dr. Albert Edward Day, a Methodist minister whose book, *Discipline and Discover*, has provided inspiration and guidelines for Christians to be more intentional in following spiritual disciplines. As I read through the book, I was most intrigued with this statement in the first chapter.

> The spiritual power of the church depends, not upon complicated organization or creative administration, important as these are; not upon eloquent preaching nor adequate theology, valuable as they are; not even upon unlimited financial resources. What the church primarily needs today, as always, is the presence of God-conscious, God-centered Christians. Even a few here and there would greatly help a church confronted by the chaos of this age.[14]

Dr. Day's insights are as appropriate and significant today as they were in 1947 when this book was first published. A few weeks later, I was still pondering the DOC invitation. A phone call came from Reverend Danny Morris, a staff member of the Upper Room Ministries, with another offer. Would I be interested in moving to Nashville and working with the Upper Room in the area of prayer and healing ministry? My book *Blessed to Be a Blessing* had prompted that call. He went on to say that Lance Webb, a retired United Methodist bishop and member of the DOC National Board of Directors, was in conversation with Maxie Dunnam. The bottom line was they were trying to work out an arrangement where I would be employed fifty-fifty, giving half my time to the DOC and half my time to the Upper Room. Danny invited Mary Lou and me to come to Nashville for an interview with Reverend Rueben Job, world editor of the Upper Room. Along with Toby, we went. Rueben was quite convincing and encouraged me to accept.

We returned to Athens with mixed emotions. We enjoyed the familiarity of pastoral ministry and questioned the uncertainty of making a major move. We prayed the increase/decrease prayer. If God's will was for us to move, then we were confident God would increase our desire to do this. If not, God would decrease our desire to accept these unsolicited offers. Also, we asked our family and close friends to add their prayers for direction and discernment. Our prayer went something like this.

> Gracious and loving God, here are two good and worthy opportunities to serve you and continue in significant ministry. If you want us to accept the invitation to move to Nashville, increase that desire within us. If not, decrease that aspiration within us. In Jesus's name, we pray. Amen.

Following several weeks of being open to God's promptings, it became clear that going to Nashville was a rare and unusual opportunity. I contacted Dwight Loder, presiding bishop of the United Methodist churches in West Ohio, asking his approval and requesting this special appointment. After having lunch with Bishop and Mrs. Loder, Mary Lou and I felt more comfortable about the move and proceeded to make it happen. Consequently, we purchased a home in Mt. Juliet, Tennessee, a suburb of Nashville. In the spring of 1984 we began this new chapter in our lives.

The next nine years were filled with innovative ministry as I began to write and develop new resources for local churches in prayer and healing ministries. The Upper Room published a revised and updated version of *Blessed to Be a Blessing,* titled *An Adventure in Healing and Wholeness* with the subtitle "The Healing Ministry of Christ in the Church Today." This book became the curriculum for training clergy and laity in developing and sustaining more intentional healing ministries in local churches. With a high interest in this ministry, I was invited to conduct training seminars and workshops in hundreds of churches throughout the United States, mostly United Methodist. However, I was also welcomed in congregations of other denominations: Presbyterian, Lutheran, Baptist, Pentecostal, Disciples of Christ, Nazarene, Roman Catholic, Mennonite, Episcopal, Church of the Brethren, Church of God, and United Church of Christ. The result was certifying 125 persons who were capable, trained, and willing to travel to other churches to teach this prayer and healing ministry model. *The Adventure in Healing and Wholeness,* also published in Korean and Hispanic languages, crossed international borders as I traveled to South Korea; Sierre Leone, West Africa; Australia; Mexico; and Europe conducting training sessions, preaching, and leading healing services.

"God's timing is always on time," as someone once noted. In 1992, the new United Methodist Book of Worship came off the press with sixteen pages devoted to healing services and special prayers. Never before in the history of Methodism in the United States had healing ministry been officially endorsed. I was invited to submit liturgies for healing services, one incorporating Holy Communion and one without the Lord's Table. These were then field tested, edited, and printed in the Book of Worship. I quote these opening lines from the introduction.

> All healing is of God. This Church's healing ministry in no way detracts from the gifts God gives through medicine and psychotherapy. It is no substitute for either medicine or the proper care of one's health. Rather, it adds to our total resources for wholeness ... God does not promise that we shall be spared suffering but does promise to be with us in our suffering ... God does not promise that we will be cured of all illnesses ... a Service of Healing is not necessarily a service of curing, but it provides an atmosphere in which healing can happen.

> The greatest healing of all is the reunion or reconciliation of a human being with God. When this happens, physical healing sometimes occurs, mental and emotional balance is often restored, spiritual health is enhanced, and relationships are healed.[15]

Here is another way to describe whole-person ministry as practiced by Jesus and described by Albert E. Day: "Health is a combination of harmonious relationships, spiritual vitality, psychological maturity, and physical wellness."[16]

And so it came about that in the late twentieth century, intentional ministries of healing and wholeness were integrated more and more into ordinary church life quietly, without fanfare, intentionally, and purposely, along with Sunday school, choirs, Bible study groups, and all the other regularly scheduled expressions of children, youth, and adult ministries. We were beginning to do what Jesus intended for us to do—that is, the threefold ministry of teaching, preaching, and healing.

Then something else was added to our church experiences—something we had not anticipated. The bishop of the Tennessee Conference of the United Methodist Church wanted to start a new church in Mt. Juliet. Reverend Jim Robinson was appointed with no church building or membership role. Not having a church home, we decided this could be a helpful and inspiring ministry. We volunteered along with twenty others. For several months, we met in the pastor's home to pray, strategize, and plan for a new church start. A storefront property was located and leased on a main thoroughfare. It certainly did not look like a church from the outside, however inside was adequate space to do church on a daily and weekly basis. Via a telephone marketing plan. we contacted hundreds of residents within our ZIP code and celebrated the first worship service with some two hundred persons in attendance. Many of these were invited guests, friends from other churches, and family members. The second Sunday, the count was more realistic, around one hundred, and then steadily grew from that point.

Starting a new church is not the easiest thing to do. Only with volunteers could we clean the restrooms, prepare the worship area each week, answer the telephone, provide secretarial assistance, and call on new families in the community. Mary Lou organized a choir, and I taught an adult Sunday school class. Along with the other members, we also took our turn with custodial duties. God blessed us with budding church leadership and frequent visitors looking for a church home. After a year or so, we met the organizational requirements, and the Mt. Juliet United Methodist Church was chartered.

My responsibilities as executive director of the Disciplined Order of Christ involved much air travel as I visited the six geographic regions of the DOC in the United States. Each region elected a board of directors and sponsored one or more spiritual retreats each year. As part of the body of Christ, the DOC works closely with local churches in becoming more committed and more effective in following Christ by pledging to live by these seven disciplines.

1.   Private daily Bible reading, meditation, and prayer.
2.   A lifestyle that focuses on obedience, simplicity, humility, frugality, generosity, truthfulness, purity, and charity.

3. Small group participation for sharing and prayer.
4. Active church membership.
5. Christian service and witness.
6. Stewardship in response to all of God's gifts.
7. Ecumenical fellowship with all Christian traditions.[17]

Perhaps the uniqueness of the DOC can be illustrated by an elderly woman who was attending a one-day retreat in Baltimore several years ago. That morning as I was leading the opening session on spiritual growth, she interrupted, saying, "What I want to know is, how do you get Christians motivated to want to grow in Christ? So many Christians I meet in my retirement community and hear on TV are stuck on spiritual obstetrics."

"What do you mean by spiritual obstetrics?" I asked.

"Well," she politely responded, "I mean those Christians who give total attention to being born again and give little or no attention to St. Paul's teachings on growing up in the mind and spirit of Christ." After a pause to think about what she had just said, she continued. "I guess what I'm asking is this, how do you get Christians to move out of the spiritual nursery and move on to spiritual maturity?" She had made her point, and all of us knew what she meant. All Christians come into a personal relationship and saving knowledge of Jesus Christ via spiritual obstetrics, a new birth of the spirit, an intentional decision, a complete reorientation of life centered not on self but on our gracious, loving, caring, merciful God. For some, this can be an often-recalled conscious moment. For others, coming to know and accept Jesus Christ is a more gradual movement of the Holy Spirit. However, that is only the first step, a baby step into the first grade of the lifelong school of learning and growing in the mind and spirit of Christ. We may be converted to Christ in the miracle of an amazing, grace-filled moment, but becoming a totally transformed, Christ-centered human being is an everyday, lifelong process.

So how does the serious Christian move out of the spiritual nursery? Here is how Maxie Dunnam answers that vital question.

> Spiritual disciplines are the ways we allow the Holy Spirit to train us to be like Jesus, to appropriate His Spirit, and to cultivate the power to live His life in the world.[18]

Christopher, when we feel, believe, or just know that Jesus is inviting us to follow him, it requires effort on our part, called discipline. Yes, that word is not very popular these days, but ponder this thought by Albert E. Day.

> Never practice discipline for its own sake. Discipline is only the means to an end; it is not the end in itself. It is the way to a vivid awareness of God and to creative communion with God.[19]

You have heard about reading readiness and math readiness. Here, I am asking you to consider spiritual readiness in your life. Whenever and wherever you become ready to move ahead in your Christian journey, do yourself and Jesus a big favor by practicing the spiritual disciplines that seem appropriate for you. You may want to discuss this with your pastor or a trusted Christian friend.

After nine years with the Upper Room Ministries and the Disciplined Order of Christ, I experienced a restlessness and wondered if Christ wanted me to stay or return to the pastoral ministry. In the spring of 1993, I wrote a letter to Judith Craig, bishop of the United Methodist Churches in West Ohio, telling her that if she had a church that needed a pastor, perhaps I might be considered. Soon came a phone call from her office informing me that Bishop Craig had received my letter and that the Fairview United Methodist Church in Dayton, Ohio, would be interviewing for a new pastor. Would Mary Lou and I be interested in meeting with the Pastor/Parish Relations Committee?

Immediately after hanging up, I phoned my wife and said, "Mary Lou, if you are not sitting down, please sit. What I am about to tell you is almost unbelievable. Bishop Craig wants us to go to Fairview Church Dayton for an interview."

"What? You have to be kidding!"

"No joke. Do you think we should go?"

Ironically, Bishop Craig did not know our history with that church. She had no idea that Mary Lou's father, Reverend Lorin Stine, had been a pastor there when she'd been a teenager. He had presided at our wedding in that church, and it was that congregation that recommended me as a candidate for ordained ministry back in the 1950s. Freda, Mary Lou's mother, was also astounded.

Again, we fervently prayed the increase/decrease prayer. The desire to leave Nashville and return to Dayton increased to the point where we agreed to go for the interview and accept whatever happened next. Everyone on the consultation committee was equally surprised. Some of them knew about our past relationship with Fairview. Before the evening was over, they invited me to come on the staff as the senior pastor starting July 1, 1993.

The next six years were challenging as I dealt with a racially changing neighborhood, economic uncertainties, an aging congregation, and a "this is the way we have always done it" mold. Discerning Christ's vision for the future of Fairview Church became a high priority. Let it also be said (and underlined) that some of the most capable, creative, faithfully committed, Christ-centered members engaged in a multitude of ministries, reaching out to the surrounding community and, along with their pastor, offering shepherding, loving care to our church family. On the last Sunday in June 1999, following forty years of ministry, I retired. One month later, Mary Lou and I moved to Galloway, Ohio, a suburb in the southwest corner of Columbus. A comfortable condo was our new home as we began the retirees chapter of our lives.

Wow, Christopher! Seems like I can hardly stop the flow of words when I get started. However, I felt you might like to know all of those comings and goings, along with some preaching and teaching tossed in. Let me hear from you real soon.

Granddaddy

Letter 6
Forgiveness

To forgive is the highest, most beautiful form of love.
In return, you will receive untold peace and happiness.
—Robert Muller

Christopher,

Apparently you have been revisiting my letter describing my experiences in the ministry of prayer and healing. Your recent e-mail poses a significant question about a critical and elusive factor in the healing process. Let me answer your inquiry this way.

Who Am I?

I am highly sought after, but strangely avoided.

I am taught faithfully to children, but rarely lived by the tutors.

I am romanticized in poem and novel, but seldom seen in everyday life.

I am first cousin to mercy and love, but all too absent in the human family.

I am related to forgetting, but not kin to amnesia.

I am a key to good health, but hardly used to unlock benefits unlimited.

I am an antidote for dealing with stress-filled relationships, but kept hidden in resentful hearts.

I am the topic of many sermons, but living examples are hard to come by.

I am not impossible, though I am perceived to be improbable and impractical.

I am understood as a vital need for everyone, but no one wants to go first.

I am called a chance to start over, a sign of hope, a medicine to cure this world's ills.

I am a gift from God for receiving and giving.

I am forgiveness![20]

Christopher, would it surprise you to know that approximately 50 percent of those who request healing prayer ask for help not for their physical pains and limitations, but rather for their spiritual, emotional, and mental anguish over damaged and fractured relationships? My experience is that those who carry deep hurts by others; harbor resentment, revenge, jealousy, anger, and hateful attitudes; or are unwilling to give or receive forgiveness have chosen to live with agonizing problems and an unwelcomed opening to personal illnesses.

Whereas forgiveness opens the door to a more satisfying life and to avenues of good health, unforgiveness keeps the door locked with a self-imposed, critical, unbending, legalistic, I-know-I'm-right-and-you-are-wrong attitude. Some people think they are doing another a favor by offering forgiveness. The truth is forgiveness blesses the giver more than it benefits the intended receiver. This is sometimes called the boomerang effect. Forgiving behavior brings positive returns to the forgiver. However, the boomerang effect is also operative when forgiveness is withheld, causing a negative impact on the unforgiver.[21]

We know from reading the gospels of Matthew, Mark, Luke, and

John that Jesus frequently taught and modeled forgiveness. The spiritual dimensions and benefits of the forgiveness process are embedded within the DNA of Christianity. I find it most encouraging that forgiveness research is a budding science outside of religious teachings, attracting increasing numbers of investigators who are motivated to explore the relationship between forgiveness and health. Current scientific studies are affirming the health potential of forgiveness. Dr. Fred Luskin, a pioneer in forgiveness research, is convinced that "learning to forgive is good for both your mental and physical well-being and your relationships."[22]

Christopher, I know this seems like more than you asked, but forgiveness and unforgiveness is quite complicated and brings up many related issues in life. For instance, the basic reason that forgiveness is difficult is because it is contrary to human nature. We are born into this world with a strong desire to protect ourselves at all costs. Watch little children at play and observe how they instinctively hit back when someone hits them or tries to take a toy away. Forgiveness is a learned response and is not instinctively employed when needed. Jesus instructs his followers to not strike back with "an eye for an eye" or "a tooth for a tooth," but rather to "turn the other cheek" when you get slapped (Matthew 5:38–39).

This means that every time you get hurt by someone (and it will happen frequently), you have to make a conscious decision what to do next. In other words, the desire to forgive is not automatic. You may have been baptized into the Christian faith, made a personal commitment to accept Jesus as your Lord and Savior, and been taught biblical principles of forgiveness, but what is your next step in a broken relationship? Do you try to get even, be mad forever, and harbor resentment, or do you try to repair the brokenness and move on with your life?

Several years ago, I discovered the teachings of Doris Donnelly, a Catholic laywoman and college professor who has written helpful books on this universal topic.[23] When I attended one of her workshops, she outlined three steps in the forgiveness process, and now I pass them on to you.

Step 1: I am hurt and upset by someone.
Step 2: I name the hurtful issue and choose to forgive.
Step 3: I attempt reconciliation.

Our basic human tendency is not to go beyond Step one. Many simply choose to ignore the problem, pout, get mad, begin plotting ways to get even, or try to smooth things over and not deal with the deeper issues involved. However, consider the time factor when choosing to move to step two. It may take five minutes, five days, five years, or longer. Time does not heal, but time offers needed space to deal with one's damaged feelings and identify what really went wrong in the relationship. To move too quickly from step one to step two is not helpful. To never move to step two is worse. I find it very beneficial to ask for the guidance of the Holy Spirit in trying to decide how I am going to express my forgiveness. Jesus taught several ways in his Sermon on the Mount (Matthew 5–7). Step three is a worthy goal, but it is not achievable if the other person does not want to work at it. We definitely make the attempt and pray for reconciliation. When it happens, we thank God for positive results. Be realistic, however. Remember the only person you have any control over is yourself. You may have to move on with your life without being reconciled.

Perhaps I can illustrate these three steps with a true story that occurred in our family when our son, Toby, was a junior in high school. As I recall the details, it went something like this. One evening we were finishing our supper, and Toby asked if he could borrow the family car to drive to the high school. He and two of his friends were asked to usher for the class play. We said, "That will be all right. Just be home before midnight. You do have school tomorrow." Toby was home in time and went straight to bed.

The next morning, I received a phone call from the high school principal informing me that Toby and his buddies did their ushering duties, but after the curtain opened, they got into areas of the building that were supposed to be off limits. Then they proceeded to put superglue in the door locks in three of their "favorite" teachers' classrooms. That morning, not having solvent for the superglue, the school could not hold class in those rooms. The principal went on to say, "The boys are being suspended from school for three days. They will have to pay for new locks. Toby is on his way home as we speak." I met Toby at the parsonage. He verified everything the principal had said.

> **Step 1:** I was hurt and upset by Toby's unacceptable behavior. I told him I would discuss it with him when we were calmed down.

Step 2: About a week later, Toby and I had a conversation about this unfortunate incident. I expressed my disappointment in his behavior; specifically, he had violated our family trust in him. We expected him to be truthful to his parents at all times—and of course, to never vandalize property and break school rules.

Step 3: Father and son reconciled. Both of us moved on.

Considering some of the major problems between parents and teenagers, this was certainly a minor incident. Yet it took his mother about one month before she was ready to move from step one to steps two and three. Each of us must deal with our personal feelings and expectations when forgiveness/unforgiveness situations call for attention.

There is so much more I could say about this complicated topic. For instance, when someone genuinely desires to let bygones be bygones or is attempting to move on in life after a personally damaging experience, a well-meaning friend might say, "Now, you just have to forgive yourself and put all this behind you." The psychologists may have some suggestions on forgiving oneself, but nowhere in the Bible are instructions given, and neither is the phrase "forgive yourself" mentioned. God mercifully and continuously offers us personal forgiveness. Self-forgiveness is the self accepting God's gracious gift of forgiveness. We always have the option of calling on God for help in all matters of forgiveness.

Another common comment related to forgiveness is, "Well, you have really not forgiven someone unless you can forget everything. Forgive and forget is the goal." My response is simply that amnesia is not our goal. We do not ask God to erase the memory tapes of our past. It is totally unrealistic to expect God to blank out certain episodes in our personal histories. The forgiveness process is complete when we can recall the hurtful person or damaging event without remembering or refeeling the pain, the injury, and the distress associate with that memory. The goal is to forgive the person and let go of the pain, but to not forget the damaging circumstances, or else we may repeat the relationship problem in the future.

Some people believe that forgiveness begins when one's emotions are ready, when more positive feelings start to surface. Forgiveness is not an act of the heart (the emotions). Rather, forgiveness begins with a decision of the mind (the intellect). If we wait until we feel like forgiving someone, we may never get around to doing it. We always have a choice, and when we consciously decide to forgive someone, it may take several days or longer for our emotions and feelings to catch up and accept what the mind chose to do.

This brings up the matter of human relations that go horribly wrong, with people being brutally victimized and severely damaged emotionally. Those situations may call for a pre-forgiveness prayer—something like this.

O God, I can't do it. I simply can't forgive_____.
I'm not even sure what to do next. Help me through this.
Help me sleep at night. Help me cope. Help me to be willing
to be willing to forgive someday—maybe not today, and
probably not tomorrow, but some day. Amen.[24]

This is step one in the pre-forgiveness process. With sincere prayer and the passage of time, it is possible (although difficult) to move on to steps two and three.

One of the realities of life is that we are sometimes blindsided and find ourselves entangled in situations causing relationship problems. For instance, for several years after I retired, we had a home in a Florida retirement community. When we decided to upgrade the kitchen, we hired a young man who was quite handy and skilled in everything that needed to be done. However, because he had a day job, he could only work on our project in the evenings and on weekends. It happened that one Saturday evening around 8:00 p.m. he was building cabinets on the carport. We were inside, totally unaware of the racket he was making outside.

Suddenly we heard a man's voice yelling loudly. Mary Lou went outside and discovered our next door neighbor on his screened-in porch highly upset over the loud noise made by the power tools. He was saying something like this: "Hey, out there. Stop that racket! We can't hear ourselves talk. Why can't you get your work done from eight to five like most people?" His tirade was peppered with words I don't care to repeat. We found out later that this man had been holding his little dog on his lap and when he started yelling, and that scared the dog, who jumped up and bit him on the face. Also, he and his friend had been consuming beer for a while.

The work stopped immediately. My first thought was, *How stupidly immature of that guy next door, yelling and making a scene like that. If there was a problem, why did he not call me on the phone or come over and knock on my door with his complaint? We would gladly have taken care of the matter.* I woke up early Sunday morning replaying that Saturday night scene in my mind, rehashing two points.

- I am responsible for hiring the kitchen remodeler.
- My neighbor was totally irresponsible for his behavior.

Enter the forgiveness process.

Step 1: I was upset and my neighbor was upset. We had a problem.

Step 2: I chose to do something about it.

In church that morning, I began to pray, not really knowing what to do next. Then slowly but surely, it came to me. I had no control over my neighbor's actions, but I could do something positive myself. I could knock on his door and apologize for disturbing his peace and quiet. Since he seldom came to Florida, I didn't even know his name.

Step Three: I attempted reconciliation. When we got home from church, I knocked on his door, not knowing what to expect. He opened the door. "Hello, I'm your neighbor, Jim Wagner. I've come to apologize for what happened last night." There was an awkward moment, and then we shook hands. He invited me in and proceeded to justify his behavior. He was calm, friendly, and offered me a beer, which I interpreted as accepting my apology. I thanked him for his gesture of hospitality but said I needed to get back home. The total length of the visit was maybe five minutes.

This story continues with an interesting twist. The next morning, I read in the *Upper Room Devotional Magazine* these words by Jesus, as recorded in Luke 6:27–28. "I tell you to love your enemies, do good to those who hate you, bless those who curse you, pray for those who mistreat you." After breakfast, I went outside to trim some bushes. Along came my neighbor, preparing to trim his bushes. We greeted each other cordially. He extended his hand and said, "I'm sorry about Saturday night. I don't know why I do those things. Guess I was not thinking straight. It won't happen again." We shook hands. I thanked him and continued trimming my bushes.

Later that afternoon, my kitchen contractor returned to build cabinets on the carport. This time the neighbor came out of his house, introduced himself, apologized for yelling, and said, "You know, I've been watching you work. You are real good at what you do. I have a friend who is looking for someone to remodel his kitchen. Can I give him your number?"

The response was, "Thanks, but no thanks. I have all the work I can handle right now." A true story!

Christopher, remember you always have a choice when it comes to disruptive relationships. When studying the life and ministry of Jesus, I am impressed that he took the initiative. By his personal example, he demonstrated what it means to forgive whenever forgiveness is called for, whether or not we feel like forgiving. When he was dying on the cross, Jesus did not wait until his persecutors apologized. He did not wait until he was feeling better before he prayed, "Father, forgive them, for they know not what they are doing" (Luke 23:34 NRSV).

If anyone had the right to be unforgiving, it was the innocent, crucified Jesus who died expressing forgiveness. I truly believe that means everyone who takes the name Christian forfeits all rights and privileges to withhold forgiveness.[25]

Christopher, I do not expect you to remember all of the intricacies of forgiveness that I have highlighted in this letter. However, you might keep it where you can reread it when an unforgiving attitude tries to take control and forgiveness seems inappropriate for whatever reason. This thoughtful insight by Henri Nouwen offers yet another perspective on the complex drama of life.

> Forgiveness is the name of love practiced among people who love poorly. The hard truth is that all of us love poorly. We do not even know what we are doing when we hurt others. We need to forgive and be forgiven every day, every

hour unceasingly. That is the great work of love among the fellowship of the weak that is the human family.[26]

I close with a note of gratitude for your questions and pray that you will pursue a forgiveness lifestyle. This prayer, penned by my friend Harry Camp, who for many years practiced law in Tennessee, is a gift to be shared.

We thank you, God of grace and mercy, for your patience with our stubbornness, for your loving consistency with our inconsistencies, for giving so generously to each of us when we are not deserving, for calling us together and helping us not only to come into new understandings of forgiveness, but also empowering us to move out of our self-imposed prisons of resentment, anger, and bitterness and into the liberating freedom of your compassion. In the name of Jesus Christ, who taught us the way to forgive and whose life revealed how to forgive. Amen.[27]

Granddaddy

Letter 7
Awaiting Further Light

Trust in the Lord with all your heart, and do not rely on your own insight.
—Proverbs 3:5 (NRSV)

Christopher,

Thank you for your positive e-mail response to my last letter, which focused on forgiveness. This leads me to address some other complex issues related to Christianity. Do I have definitive and final answers? No, but I can share with you my understandings and experiences in living with these daunting questions. Before we get into that, let me tell you what I am certain about.

I recall one evening when I was nine or ten years old and playing outside. While lying down on the grass, I looked up into the night sky and wondered, "Since God made the moon and all those stars, how can God even know I'm here?" Then not too long after that, I discovered Psalm 8:3–4 (NRSV).

> When I look at your heavens, the work of your fingers, the moon and the stars that you have established; what are human beings that you are mindful of them, mortals that you care for them?

Coupled with John 3:16 (NRSV), one of the most quoted verses in the New Testament, I was beginning to see a connection to my boyhood curiosity.

> For God so loved the world that he gave his only Son, so that everyone who believes in him may not perish but may have eternal life.

When I spoke my confirmation vows in church around age twelve, I made a personal commitment to Jesus and to follow his way of life. Since then every time I participate in the Sacrament of Holy Communion, the Spirit of Jesus is present and personal. A question often asked is, "What is a Christian?" One of the best answers comes from Dr. Elton Trueblood: "A Christian is a person who, with all the honesty of which he or she is capable, becomes convinced of the trustworthiness of Jesus Christ."[28]

Because this commitment needs to be consciously renewed each day, in recent years I have developed the habit of taking time for silence and solitude (usually before breakfast), for Bible study, lifting names of others needing help and healing, reading from devotional classics, and centering-listening prayer. Being a committed and active Christian develops a foundation and a positive place to stand when confronted by challenges that surface along our spiritual journeys.

Perhaps you have heard it said, "Just when I think I have the answer, someone changes the question." Here are some that I continue to ponder.

1. Why Are Not All Sick People Healed?

When I was conducting seminars on the healing ministry of the church, this question was frequently asked. My initial response has been to affirm God's desire for all human beings to have good health in body, mind, spirit, and relationships, citing four kinds of evidence.

- In the Book of Genesis 1:31 (NRSV), creation is described as being "very good." God provides a healthy environment for humankind on planet Earth.
- The human body consistently heals itself. When our illnesses need help in the healing process, doctors use medicine, surgery, and various therapies that are intended to cooperate with the body's battle against disease and sickness.
- Medical research and discoveries of the health care professions continue to alleviate human suffering and offer cures for many illnesses that were labeled incurable at one time.
- The active and intentional healing ministry of Jesus in the four Gospels is a powerful witness to God's desire for whole person

health. Note this emphasis in Matthew 9:35–36 (NRSV). "Jesus traveled among all the cities and villages, teaching in their synagogues, announcing the good news of the kingdom, and healing every disease and every sickness. When Jesus saw the crowds he had compassion on them."

This is the rationale for my personal belief that God is a healing, loving, caring creator who desires (wills) health, wholeness, and salvation for everyone. However, God's desires are often blocked and not always accomplished because God has given each of us free will to do, act, and think as we choose. If God did not permit us to function in life with freedom in decision making, we would be little more than marionettes on God's celestial string. Herein lies the agony and ecstasy of belonging to the human race. Because God does not predetermine every step you and I take in life, we have unlimited possibilities for bad and good, sickness and health, death and life.[29]

This means that when I pray for healing for myself or for another person, I am expressing my deep desire to cooperate with God in the healing process. Jesus proved to us that God is on the side of good health. My experience in healing ministry is that when physical illness is not cured, God blesses in other ways. Those who ask, "Why are all people not healed?" usually mean physical healing. The popular mindset sees physical health as the essence of life and ignores a holistic view, disregarding spiritual health, mental health, emotional health, and healthy human relationships. God is faithful and brings us blessings, benefits, and improvements in other areas of our being when the physical self weakens.[30]

I agree with Dr. Albert E. Day, who reminds us that in discussing healing ministry, we tend to recite the worst case scenario. However, he points out that if we can name one person whose health situation definitely improved when the best spiritual therapy was combined with the best medical therapy, that should be motivation enough to keep on keeping on as faithful, compassionate disciples of the healing Christ.

Of this much I am certain: some for whom we pray will experience a physical healing that could not otherwise have been their happy lot; others will enter a blessed, conscious comradeship with God. But all will know that the church and its ministers deeply care for them, feel their pain, and share their grief. The church will become a fellowship of those who bear the marks of pain, which is strangely enough a fellowship of unique joy.[31]

2. Why Does God Allow Suffering?

I believe that God does not intentionally cause suffering, be it from natural disasters, human sinfulness, or seemingly incurable disease and illness. Suffering does not happen to teach us something or to punish us, but often occurs in unpredictable ways beyond our control. The will of God has more to do with how we respond to suffering than with how and why life too often deals unfairly and unjustly with us and our larger world. These biblical guidelines and proven blessings taught by Apostle Paul in his early churches continue to serve us well in the twenty-first century.

> We know that all things work together for good for those who love God, who are called according to his purpose. (Romans 8:28 NRSV)

> Do not worry about anything, but in everything by prayer and supplication with thanksgiving let your requests be made known to God. And the peace of God, which surpasses all understanding, will guard your hearts and your minds in Christ Jesus. (Philippians 4:6–7 NRSV)

So why are not all people healed? In many situations, I am still looking for answers. However, as I heard the famed faith healer Reverend Oral Roberts say, "I have prayed for healing with more people who were not healed than with those who were healed. Nevertheless, I want to be faithful and compassionate to all and in all."[32]

3. Why Did Jesus Die on a Cross?

Throughout the history of the Church, Christians have made many attempts to unravel and explain the mystery and message of Jesus's death on a cross. These are called theories of atonement. A theory is designed to help us understand what appears to be beyond our limited understanding.

Yet the human mind is so curious and investigative that intelligent people want to know the why, who, when, and how of things and events. The word *atonement* is recorded in four places in the New Testament and means harmony or reconciliation between God and humankind.[33]

Christopher, you may think that it is a no-brainer to even raise this question: Why did Jesus die on a cross? Are we not taught in church that he died for our sins? Yes, but the four Gospels and Paul's writings in the New Testament do not give a single consistent answer to that question. Consider these various theories of atonement.

1. Ransom Theory: The main explanation of the crucifixion for the first one thousand years of church history. Jesus's death was kind of a transaction between God and the devil. To release the devil's hold on humanity, Jesus paid the full price and achieved supreme and eternal victory over sin and death. As recorded in Mark 10:45, "The son of man came not to be served but to serve, and to give his life as a ransom for many." So we by faith in Christ likewise share in victory over sin and death. However, the devil was tricked by God, whose trump card was the resurrection of Jesus Christ on what we now call Easter Sunday.

2. Substitution Theory: A widely held theory throughout Christianity. Christ did for us what we could not do for ourselves—namely, pay our sin debt to God. By taking our sins and the sins of the world upon himself, Christ satisfied divine justice. In Romans 5:8–9, Paul declares, "God proves his love for us, because while we still were sinners Christ died for us. Much more surely then, now that we have been justified by his blood will we be saved through him from the wrath of God."

3. Moral Influence Theory: Christ's death on a cross serves as the ultimate example for us to lead lives of sacrificial love. This concept emphasizes not a wrathful, vengeful God but a merciful, forgiving, loving God who took the initiative through his special Son, Jesus, to reach out to all humankind. Reflect on these significant words of Jesus: "And I, when I am lifted up from the earth, will draw all

people to myself." He said this to indicate the kind of death he was to die (John 12:32–33). This is sometimes called the Magnet Atonement Theory because the message of the cross from the one who died on a cross continues to be an unavoidable attraction.

This is only a sampling of human attempts to understand and explain the message and purpose of the crucifixion. Other atonement theories abound. This comment by Richard Rohr deserves our attention.

> The cross is not the price that Jesus had to pay to talk God into loving us. It is simply where love will lead us. Jesus names the agenda. If we love, if we give ourselves to feel the pain of the world, it will crucify us. This understanding of the crucifixion is much better than thinking of Jesus as paying some debt to an alienated God who needs to be talked into loving us.[34]

Biblical scholars and theologians continue to ponder and publish books on the question, "Why did Jesus die on a cross?" I encourage you to pursue this on your own in prayer, conversation with other Christians, and further study. I will be sending you a recommended bibliography. Books by Leslie Weatherhead have been especially helpful for me. Here is his insight regarding the will of God, a phrase we easily say and pray but seldom comprehend.

- The intentional will of God: this is God's ideal desires and yearnings for human beings.
- The circumstantial will of God: within changing circumstances due to human free-will God continues to be concerned and active.
- The ultimate will of God: The final realization of God's purposes.

In applying this concept to the cross of Jesus, Weatherhead goes on to say, "It was not the intentional will of God, surely, that Jesus should be crucified, but that Jesus should be followed. If the nation had understood and received his message, repented of its sins, and realized his kingdom, the history of the world would have been different. The crucifixion was the will of evil-minded men, not the will of God. But when Jesus was faced with the circumstances brought on by evil and was thrust into the dilemma of running away or being crucified, then in those circumstances, the cross became his Father's will. It was in this sense that Jesus prayed, "Father, for you all things are possible; remove this cup from me; yet, not what I want, but what you want" (Mark 14:36 NRSV).

In the case of the cross, the ultimate will of God means that the high goal of humankind's redemption and recovery of unity with God—a goal that would have been reached by God's intentional plan had it not been frustrated—may still be reached through his circumstantial will. In a sentence, no evil is finally able to defeat God.[35]

I believe Jesus died not fully realizing the power for salvation, reconciliation, and wholeness of health in body, mind, and spirit that would come into the world because of his cross and resurrection. This is why that horribly bad day on which Jesus died, Christians now call it Good Friday.

Christopher, here are some other intriguing questions I continue to ponder.

- What about those who die without accepting Jesus Christ as their Lord and Savior? Does God provide more opportunities after physical death?
- What about the millions of people who follow non-Christian beliefs and traditions (such as Judaism, Islam, Buddhism, Hinduism) and who claim theirs is the true religion?
- What was Jesus doing with his life between ages twelve and thirty?
- What will life in heaven be like?
- The return of Christ in final victory is repeatedly stated in the New Testament. When and how might that happen?
- What evidence do we have that Christ actually arose from the dead—a miraculous phenomenon that we celebrate each year on Easter Sunday?

Here is my personal thinking on this last question. If the Church depended only on human leadership, Christianity would have caved in centuries ago. Throughout the ups and downs of Church history, it has been and will continue to be the leadership of the risen Christ, who is the head of the body, the Church, who holds it all together and offers spiritual renewal and abundant life without ceasing. For me, the existence of the Christian religion into the twenty-first century is authentic evidence of Christ's resurrection. Or as my daughter Kerrie said it when she was about four years old and we were discussing the meaning of Easter, "Well, he didn't stay dead."

Christopher, that's about it for now. I'm sure you wrestle with your own perplexing questions. Rather than stubbornly trying to solve all the puzzles of life, sometimes it is better to kick back, relax, and simply live into the questions. I leave you with a wise word from one of my seminary professors. One day in class, a student asked Dr. J. Arthur Heck to interpret a difficult verse in the Bible. His response was, "I do not have a ready answer to that question, but I will tell you what I do whenever I come across anything in the Bible that challenges my understanding. I simply pencil in the margin beside the verse: 'Awaiting further light.'"

Make that your own practice and see what might result.

Granddaddy

Letter 8
Living in the Fourth Quarter

What we once loved and deeply enjoyed we can never
lose, for all that we love deeply becomes part of us.
—Helen Keller

Christopher,

When people talk about how old they are and begin to reflect seriously on
their life's journey, they sometimes divide their years into four seasons:
spring, summer, autumn, and winter. Some view their experiences similar to
a play in four acts. Personally, I think about my life as moving in and through
four distinct quarters. The first quarter is ages 1–25, the second quarter is
ages 25–50, the third quarter is ages 50–75, and the fourth quarter is ages
75 and older. These are not necessarily precise, and there could well be some
overlap. However, now that I am fully into my fourth quarter I totally agree
with Richard L. Morgan, who coined the phrase "No wrinkles on the soul."[36]
Although my body is captive to the aging process and my memory is not
what it used to be, my spiritual self has never been more alive and sensitive to
God's promptings. Living in the fourth quarter may mean retirement from
one's working years, but it certainly does not delete or slow down spiritual
nourishment and ministry opportunities. I am discovering that God always
has something more for each of us that enhances our lives and the lives of
those around us.

One of my favorite hymns says it best.

> Great is thy faithfulness, O God my Father,
> there is no shadow of turning with thee;
> Thou changest not, thy compassions, they fail not;

as thou hast been, thou forever wilt be.
All I have needed thy hand hath provided;
great is thy faithfulness, Lord, unto me.[37]

This was also one of your Nana's favorite hymns, one she often chose to sing when leading church choirs and worship experiences. Being raised in a parsonage, Mary Lou had memorized dozens of hymns. In fact when Nana had difficulty going to sleep at night, she would silently think about hymn titles alphabetically before dozing off.

Christopher, although I have mentioned Nana in our previous letters, I want to share with you some things you may not know. She was born in Rochester, Indiana, on November 3, 1934, the only child of Reverend Lorin and Freda Stine. In 1948 the family moved to Dayton, Ohio, where her father was appointed senior pastor of the Fairview EUB Church, and she began her freshman year at Fairview High School. Even though Nana had no sisters or brothers, she learned to accept and love foster children who came to live with her family from time to time. Her parents frequently entertained visitors from other countries, as well as missionaries home on furlough. Consequently, Nana was well schooled in social graces and hospitality.

Having taken piano lessons throughout her early and teenage years, she continued her interest in music at Otterbein College, majoring in piano and music education courses. She was well prepared and motivated to lead children, youth, and adult choirs in several churches where I was appointed as pastor. During my three years at United Theological Seminary, it was Nana's salary as a music teacher in the Dayton Public School System that kept us financially afloat.

Nana's Christian faith was well nourished by participating in Bible study, church music workshops, and training events for small groups and retreat leadership. After completing the Academy for Spiritual Formation, a two-year course sponsored by the Upper Room ministries, Nana was invited to lead music and worship in numerous spiritual formation events. Among other blessings, these experiences served to deepen her appreciation for the Sacrament of Holy Communion. When Nana retired from teaching school, she opened a Christian book and gift store called The Sign of the Fish. Her motivation was to augment our family income, which was being strained at the time with our two daughters in college. Her brief ownership proved to be a valuable learning experience even though profits were small. She had strong political and social justice opinions, expressed herself well when addressing groups small and large, and often spoke extemporaneously (a trait she inherited from her preacher father).

Also embedded within Nana's DNA was genuine compassion for the wounded and the marginalized. I well recall her initiating and developing friendship with two women not related to each other who were constant complainers, avid worriers, and mad about almost everything and everybody, including God. As Nana took time to listen, to care, and to pray for these reclusive neighbors, they began to reciprocate by befriending her—a slow process with rewarding outcomes. During our time in Athens, Ohio, Nana volunteered each week at The Gathering Place. This was a safe, welcoming, and friendly environment for mentally challenged adults to gather for help with medications, affordable housing, socialization skills, food preparation and cooking, personal financial issues, and group and one-on-one counseling. Later, after moving to Nashville, Nana was employed as the spiritual director for a holistic healing facility that focused on persons with closed-head injuries (usually from strokes or concussions). Several times she brought clients, who had little or no family support, home for the weekend. Nana's personal ministry with the "least and the lost" continued to blossom and bear fruit after we retired and were on the leadership team that initiated the United Methodist Church for All People, an inner-city church in Columbus, Ohio. Her genuine reaching out and personal interest in all who came for any reason into that uniquely diverse congregation went well beyond race, gender, creed, and economic and educational levels. Nana's influence helped shape this call to worship, proclaimed every Sunday.

Leader: God's love is deep and wide.

Community: God loves all people.

Leader: Beyond differences that may divide us ...

Community: No matter who we are or what we have done, we are all beloved children of God.

Leader: We are a church for all people.

Community: We give our love to everyone, no matter who they are or what they have done. Welcome to this circle![38]

Living with Nana presented several hurdles in our early years of marriage, primarily because of our different backgrounds and family values. Did we argue and quarrel? Rarely. However, we often had opposite opinions on day-to-day family matters. One that I will always remember is Nana's lack of cooking skills during those first months after the honeymoon. Undaunted by meal planning and preparation, she simply opened one of several cookbooks we had received as wedding gifts. Her position was, "If you can read, you can follow the directions and cook." One day she decided to make a pot of chili, her first time ever. After dinner she said, "Well, how do you like my chili?"

My response was, "Oh, it was okay. Not like my mother's, but okay."

About ten years later, I said to Nana one day, "We haven't had chili for a while. Why don't you make that for dinner?"

She replied, "Why don't you call your mother and ask her to make it?" Actually, Nana developed highly regarded culinary skills, as attested by her recipes appearing in published cookbooks.

Another incident that reveals something of Nana's opinionated thinking and assertive behavior occurred one December when living in Tennessee on our five-acre rural property that included hundreds of native cedar trees. These were medium-size evergreens perfectly suitable for decorating at Christmas time. With bow saw in hand, I announced that I was going up the back hill and select a tree for our living room. An hour or so later, I returned with the tree and proudly showed it to Nana on the front porch. Her response? "That is not the tree we want to bring in the house. It's too skinny and lopsided. Go get another one."

I said, "Mary Lou, if you don't like this tree, here's the saw. You go get another one." So she did. Her tree went in the living room and was beautifully decked out for our Christmas celebrations. My tree remained on the front porch with a few ornaments and a strand of lights.

As you can imagine, money was always tight, and we had to carefully budget our financial resources. That changed somewhat after we both retired and were living comfortably on our sources of income. At the same time, Nana was drawing a modest monthly social security check, which she decided was "her money" to spend as she pleased and was not to be counted on to pay our bills. She set up a personal checking account with direct deposit. Whenever she needed cash, she would make a withdrawal at the bank and put the money in a yellow plastic, zippered purse featuring a young girl and boy skipping rope with "Dick and Jane" in large letters. This became her go-to cache for nonessential yet highly enjoyable spending (birthdays, anniversaries, Christmas, eating out, any special celebration, and of course clothing items on sale).

Nana coped with multiple health issues most of her adult life. I believe it was her Christian faith and utter joy in spending time with her family, especially the grandchildren, that kept her going through increasingly difficult days. Everything came to a head on March 23, 2014, when Nana experienced a severe stroke while napping in our living room. My 911 call quickly brought the ambulance. The emergency crew took her to the stroke recovery unit at Mt. Carmel West Hospital, Columbus, Ohio. Within twenty-four hours the highly skilled and efficiently trained medical staff had a care plan in place. Although Nana had no lingering paralysis or speech loss, other impairments surfaced.

One thing that was never lost throughout this ordeal was her sense of humor. The second day in the hospital, she called for her good friends David and Joyce Warner to visit. She asked David to bring his guitar and play "You Are My Sunshine." This impromptu concert was well received not only by the patient and her family but also by the on-duty nursing staff. Once while having a medical procedure, Nana told the attending physician that she was going to play a little game with him. She would whistle a hymn or a song and ask him to name that tune.

When Nana discovered that most of the male transport staff were single, pre-med students, she would tell them about her "eligible" granddaughter who was soon to graduate from college. Her matchmaking did not Bingo, but it did bring lots of smiles within that large medical complex.

The hospital therapists and medical team had Nana ahead of the projected healing timeline. After four weeks, she was moved to an excellent rehab facility, Darby Glenn in Hilliard, Ohio, where she continued to make noticeable progress. Nana was released and returned to our home on May

9. Soon we had scheduled physical, occupational, speech therapists, and visiting nurses coming several times each week. We also made regular appointments with our longtime family physician, Dr. John Cocumelli, who monitored medications and all the procedures ordered by specialty doctors. Nana's balance was still unstable, even with the help of a walker. Unfortunately, one night while attempting to walk to the bathroom from our bedroom, she fell and suffered fractured ribs, a broken wrist, and multiple bruises. This proved to have a negative impact on her overall health.

For several years, Nana had been routinely examined for elevated liver enzymes and treated with prescription drugs. During the summer months, hospital and lab tests detected serious liver dysfunction. Then on September 9, while keeping an appointment with Dr. Anthony Michaels, gastroenterologist on the staff at the Ohio State University Hospital, we were given the diagnosis: sclerosis of the liver, non-alcohol related. Because of Nana's age, she was not eligible for a liver transplant, and there was nothing medically that could reverse the liver disease. When I asked the doctor for his prognosis, he haltingly said, "I'm very sorry. Mary Lou probably has a few weeks or months left." After thanking him for his personal concern and for taking care of Mary Lou for several years, we went for a late lunch at one of our favorite Chinese restaurants.

Nana's energy and strength began to weaken. Our children and grandchildren came on the weekends to help all they could, and simply having them in our home was good medicine. I also employed professional caregivers to be present five nights a week. Early in October, Dr. Cocumelli recommended in-home hospice care. Words cannot express our appreciation for the hospice team. They were so competent and compassionate, a Godsend in every way. We were also blessed by loving attention from our pastors, church family, good friends, and helpful neighbors. During those somber days, Toby, Kerrie, Laurie, and their families gave Nana abundant personal attention. Did Nana experience pain and discomfort in the midst of all this downturn? Some, but her pain was manageable. However, through it all, her mind was clear, and her spirit radiated love and appreciation for blessings unlimited. Nana and I frequently shared devotional readings and prayed mostly for other people who were having difficult days. Several times she told me that she was making a mental list of all the family members and friends she would be with in heaven.

When the visiting nurse recommended that Nana be transferred to a hospice facility for around-the-clock professional care, we readily agreed. During her third day at the Highbanks Care Center in Worthington, Ohio, on October 22, 2014, Nana died peacefully two weeks before her eightieth birthday, surrounded by her tearful family, who were so grateful to be with each other and with Nana as she transitioned into her next life. Three days later, everyone in our family, all twenty-six of us, gathered at the Fairview Cemetery in Galion, Ohio, for Nana's committal service, so ably led by our good friend Reverend Dan Kiger. It happened to be a gorgeous autumn morning, a perfect setting to sing "Hymn of Promise."

> In our end is our beginning; in our time, infinity;
> In our doubts there is believing; in our life eternity.
> In our death, a resurrection; at the last, a victory,
> Unrevealed until its season, something God alone can see.[39]

Kerrie's home church, First United Methodist in Crestline, Ohio, hosted our family and friends luncheon, followed by a photo shoot. I was especially blessed to have Catherine Wagner (daughter of Toby and Leslie) in the family picture, standing straight and tall in her US Air Force uniform (something of a miracle for her to be present because she was in training at Ft. Sam Houston, Texas).

As the children and I planned Nana's memorial service, our first choice was to have it at the United Methodist Church for All People, where she was one of the charter members. However, we anticipated a large attendance and needed a more spacious sanctuary. We arranged with Pastor Nathan Custer to host the service at the Columbia Heights United Methodist Church, not far from our home in Galloway, Ohio. That turned out to be a wise decision: over three hundred came to remember and honor Mary Lou Wagner on All Saints Day, November 1, 2014. In the midst of our grief, God blessed us in many ways: being surrounded by so many of her friends, special music by Kyle and Bethany Zeuch and Molly Mustaqueen, celebrating the Sacrament of Holy Communion, and the sensitive and comforting leadership of Reverend Nathan Custer, Reverend John Edgar, and Reverend Karen Cook.

Christopher, I want to share with you a portion of your Aunt Kerrie's tribute to her mother.

Several years ago, a friend gave me a devotional book called Jesus Calling. The reading for each day is a meditation written as if Jesus is speaking based on the selected scriptures. I shared this book with Mother, and it became very meaningful to both of us. Here is a part of the devotional for October 22, the day that Mother died.

> No matter what your circumstances may be, you can find joy in My Presence. On some days joy is generously strewn along your life-path, glistening in the sunlight. On days like that, being content is as simple as breathing the next breath or taking the next step. Other days are overcast and gloomy, you feel the strain of the journey which seems endless ... Yet joy is still attainable. Search for it as for hidden treasure.[40]

This reminded me of how Mother lived her life. She truly found joy in all circumstances and she made it her business to share that joy and the love of God with everyone she met each day of her life.

Also, for your family records, here are my personal words spoken at your Nana's memorial service.

> Several years ago, I met a British Methodist minister who was also a medical doctor. Mondays through Fridays, he worked in his doctor's office treating hundreds of patients. Then on weekends, he was the pastor to his congregation near London. One evening I heard the Reverend Dr. Reginald Mallett preach a sermon on the theme "When Healing Does Not Happen." To illustrate, he told the story of his sister, who lived with a life-threatening illness for an extended time. She had received the best medical care available, along with prayer therapy, within the context of loving family and caring friends. However, nothing helped her get better. Her healing did not happen, meaning her

physical healing did not happen. Then the preacher said something I have never forgotten, and I pass it on whenever I have the opportunity.

> Sometimes the body does not respond to medical help, but always remember that when the container is hopelessly flawed the contents can be wonderfully healthy and whole.[41]

Over the years, Mary Lou's container, her physical body, had endured breast cancer, a broken back, two corneal transplants, atrial fibrillation (rapid heartbeat), congestive heart problems, pneumonia, kidney and bladder infections, a severe stroke, and liver disease. By any definition or description, her container was hopelessly flawed. Nevertheless, the contents, that which makes Mary Lou a unique child of God, was and is wonderfully healthy and whole.

During the past several months, many of you here today offered prayer for Mary Lou. Were you prayers answered? For healing of her physical container, the answer is no. Today I am reminding myself and you that Mary Lou was blessed and was helped by our prayers. She was at peace with her situation. Her relationships with her family and her friends were more deeply bonded in love. Her emotional strength never wavered. Her spiritual health soared to new heights. I would say that in many ways, my wife was the spiritual head of our family—a title she would never claim, yet one she filled easily and frequently.

Several of you have expressed your personal appreciation for the positive impact that Mary Lou had on your lives. Let me tell you a secret. In going through Mary Lou's desk, file folders, and personal stuff, I found dozens of notebooks filled with handwritten prayers and list upon list of people she prayed for. Be assured that many of you were named in her intercessory prayers, some more than once. Several of you commented that you have never attended a memorial service that included the Sacrament of Holy Communion. So why now? The Lord's Supper, or Eucharist, is the most Christ-centered worship experience for Christians of all denominations and traditions. Mary Lou never wanted to miss church on Sundays when Holy Communion was offered. During the past several months, when she was not able to go to church, we would have Holy Communion in her hospital room or with her in the rehab or nursing facility. Quite often she and I would have a time of Holy Communion at our breakfast table. The secret of Mary Lou's positive influence on each of us is her deep and abiding faith in Jesus, frequenting the Lord's table, and having time alone with God in scripture, meditation, and prayer. If she were standing here today she would say to each of us, "Go thou and do likewise." This is why I am convinced that even though Mary Lou's container was hopelessly flawed, her contents were wonderfully healthy and whole.

Later, when I began to reflect on those traumatic moments, grief came calling. Some may think that a truly religious person does not grieve, or that if our faith is strong, then grief will not linger when a loved one dies. Wrong! Grief is a God-given gift to help us cope with the passing of someone who was faithfully and deeply loved. Sorrow and sadness are natural responses to personal loss. But, as Apostle Paul put it so well, "So that you may not grieve as others do who have no hope" (1 Thessalonians 4:13 NRSV). In another epistle, he offers this reassuring word of hope.

> So we do not lose heart. Even though our outer nature is wasting away, our inner nature is being renewed day by day ... for what can be seen is temporary, but what cannot be seen is eternal. For we know that if the earthly tent (container) we live in is destroyed, we have a building from

God, a house not made with hands, eternal in the heavens. (2 Corinthians 4:16–5:1 NRSV)

Yes, Christopher, I grieve every day for my companion of fifty-eight years. However, my rock-bottom belief, based on the resurrection of Jesus Christ, is that death of the body is not the end but a transition to life beyond this earthly existence. Even though the details of what God has prepared are vastly unknown, we have the option of getting stuck in our grief or moving ahead in life.

I can relate to this story about a woman who asked a psychologist, "What is grief?"

He responded, "Grief is an expression of love, and when you grieve, you allow yourself to love again."

Then she asked, "But how do you grieve?"

He replied, "You grieve and celebrate a person's life by living your life fully." This may not alleviate the loneliness, but I know it gives God more opportunities to make a positive difference.

Recently, while walking on a monastery retreat path, I came across these motivating words: "For all that was, give thanks; for all that is yet to be say yes."

In the Apostles' Creed is this statement: "I believe in the communion of saints." Nana and I often discussed this faith concept, which we affirmed wholeheartedly. The word *saints* in this context implies everyone living and deceased who has taken the name Christian when baptized and who is a committed follower of Jesus. From the root of the word *communion* are the words *community* and *communication*. Do the saints in heaven communicate with the saints on earth? Yes, I believe they do. On August 9, 2015, I had a dream about Nana—one of the most vivid dreams I have ever had. It was so real that when I woke up, I recalled the details and wrote it down.

> Mary Lou and I were together, in a car, in a big city. We stopped for gas, and when I got out of the car, she drove off alone. I went looking for her everywhere. I found her sitting peacefully at home on a sofa with her mother, Freda, and some close friends. She looked at me and did not say anything, but she gave a great big smile. Immediately I burst

into uncontrollable weeping and began to hug her dearly.
The next thing I knew, we were all seated at a banquet table
loaded with above-average food. Then I woke up.

As I processed this unusual experience, I thought about the many
occasions in the Bible where God communicated with people in visions
and dreams. I am telling you all of this simply to say that since that dream,
I have been at peace and more settled about losing Mary Lou. Now I truly
believe she is also at peace and doing okay in her new life with her beloved
parents and good friends. And the best way for me to honor and remember
Mary Lou is to move on in my own life, following Jesus, loving our family,
and being open to the nudging and leading of God's Holy Spirit. Have I had
other dreams focusing on Mary Lou? Yes, as have other family members.
Talking about these dream experiences has been reassuring.

As my friend and author Flora Wuellner states in sharing her personal
convictions,

> I do not believe God ever intended for bodily death to be
> a total separation. It is a grief, an immeasurable loss when
> the body of our loved one dies. We cannot minimize or
> trivialize that anguished sense of loss, knowing we will no
> longer hear the voice we love, the laughter, the footsteps.
> But we are so much more than our bodily selves. Our deep
> souls need never to be separated. Our love and thoughts
> can still flow to one another and mingle. All dimensions
> of heaven and earth are held alive within the heart of God,
> who is the "God not of the dead, but of the living" (Mark
> 12:27 NRSV).[42]

Well, Christopher, now you know much more about your beloved Nana
and the influence she had and continues to have on all of us within her
sphere of relationships. She dearly loved you and all of her grandchildren. As
a way of remembering this, you might want to jot down this country western
song title: "You Come from a Long Line of Love."

Granddaddy

Letter 9
Looking For Some Wisdom

You should treat people in the same way that you want
people to treat you; this is the Law and the Prophets.
—Matthew 7:12 (CEB)

Granddaddy,

Thank you for sharing so many things about you and our family that are helping me appreciate my roots and legacy. However, I am troubled these days by all the social upheaval, rampant terrorism, and unending violence, even in my corner of the world. I have friends who are Hispanic, Muslim, Jewish, black, and atheist. My friends in the LGBTQ community fear that hatred toward them will become normalized. They are some of the best people I know. They have values and live good lives. I really care and try to support them, but it doesn't seem like I am doing enough. What are some things that I can do to not standby idly? When I have grandchildren, I want to be able to tell them that I believed in something and did something about injustice. I'm wondering if you see any similarities in today's happenings as compared to the Civil Rights movement in the 1960's? I know you were an active Pastor during those uncertain and explosive times. What were some ways you dealt with all that? Just looking for some wisdom.

Christopher

Your letter deserves a thoughtful and unhurried response. Yes, these really are troubled and scary times. A multitude of factors seem to be working against "peace on earth, goodwill to all." You asked about comparisons to the 1960s social issues. I well remember that daunting era and will share some personal experiences. Racial tensions and inequalities were highlighted when over two hundred thousand people marched in Washington, DC, on August 28, 1963, to call attention to the political and social challenges African Americans faced across the country. Several minister friends decided to go and offered me an invitation and a ride. Regretfully, I decided to stay home. That massive assembly and Dr. Martin Luther King, Jr.'s "I Have a Dream" speech became a historical turning point. The next year, the Civil Rights Act of 1964 was passed in the US Congress, expressly banning discrimination based on race, color, religion, sex, or national origin. That included equal application of voter registration and desegregation in public schools.

Because this new human rights legislation was not quickly enforced throughout the land, we witnessed waves of violence, massive property damage, and lives lost. At that time, I was a pastor in Kettering, Ohio (an all-white suburb of Dayton). The east-side black ghetto of Dayton erupted. Militant black leaders emerged, demanding justice on their own terms. Several downtown churches in Dayton were robbed at gunpoint during the Sunday services, taking the morning offerings. Early one Sunday, I called an emergency meeting of our church leaders to devise a plan, just in case we were assaulted. We never were. It was totally unsettling to see the Ohio National Guard with full armor patrolling the streets of Dayton.

Obviously the violence, disruption, and threats were caused by a minority of black Americans. What could we do to help stabilize the situation and show our support for the majority? Untold numbers of interracial meetings were held for prayer, open dialogue, and restoring peace with justice. Mary Lou, never a shrinking violet, began to organize interracial gatherings for women's groups in all-black and all-white congregations. Carloads of our women met in black churches and held reciprocating events in our church. A question frequently asked was, "What are some other things we could do that might make a positive difference in our families and churches?"

Our two daughters were in a grade school where no persons of color attended. We enrolled them in swimming classes at the downtown YWCA in Dayton, thinking they would get to know black girls their own age and develop some personal relationships. Guess what? The swim classes were all-white. The order to desegregate public schools meant busing black children to white neighborhood schools and white children to black schools. Protests by parents led to unsafe conditions for children attempting to board the buses. Consequently, local pastors and priests got involved by assisting at bus stops and riding the buses.

In 1967 a ground-breaking movie came out: *Guess Who's Coming to Dinner.* A widowed black physician and a white woman from a successful and wealthy family fell in love. Her father, a newspaper publisher, and her mother, the owner of an art gallery, went ballistic when their daughter brought her fiancé home to meet the parents. One Sunday evening each month, we met with five other couples in our homes for discussions of various topics, chosen by the host couple. When it came our turn, Mary Lou and I recommended that we all go to see this movie and then gather in the parsonage to discuss it. That evening turned out to be a memorable event. Here was a room full of Christians raising their voices in loud disagreement and with little consensus over the boldness of the movie, the propaganda promoting interracial marriage, and the possibility of changing accepted cultural norms.

The Kettering Ministerial Association decided to promote open housing. We wanted to encourage black families to move into our neighborhoods. I agreed to sign my name to a full-page open letter to the Kettering community that appeared in our local newspaper. This was my personal decision. However, some church members were more than irate to see their pastor's name on this public statement, which was not an endorsement by the congregation. One member, a successful real estate agent, made an appointment to set me straight. His main argument was simply, "If blacks start moving into Kettering, all housing values will fall, and the real estate market will never recover." He threatened to leave the church, but he never did.

An unforgettable incident related to the turbulent 1960s occurred on a Sunday evening when I took a couple carloads of teenagers from our youth fellowship to see and hear Dr. Martin Luther King Jr. give a speech at the University of Dayton, only a ten-minute drive from our church. What a rare opportunity for them to experience this history-making, poster icon for the Civil Rights movement. However, the next day, more than one parent called in, most upset that their pastor would expose their children to this controversial rabble-rouser. A few weeks later, Dr. King was assassinated in Memphis, Tennessee.

Another component of those chaotic times was the Vietnam situation. In 1964, the US Congress, at the urging of the president, declared war against the North Vietnamese government. American public opinion became decidedly mixed and heated. Open protests escalated when over two million US military personnel served in Vietnam. Several thousand never came home. The last American troop left Vietnam in 1973, with historians still debating who lost or won. On the home front college and university campuses erupted, as student and faculty protestors conducted extended sit-ins, burned buildings, and confronted the National Guard. A female student was fatally shot on the campus of Kent State University.

Have we made any progress in the United States advancing civil rights and changing ingrained racial attitudes in the last fifty years? In many ways, the answer is yes. However, this letter to the editor of the *Dayton Daily News* in Ohio, published February 11, 2017, is evidence that racism is still very much with us today.

> Ten students from Stivers School for the Arts (mostly black) boarded a public bus at the end of their school day. A white woman spoke in a loud voice to her friend, "They need another bus for these people, because they take up too much room and they're loud." To the students she said, "There's room in the back of the bus. Why don't you go sit there?" Then she said to one of the white students, "Honey, I'm not talking about you. You're fine." Racism, ingrained in the culture and systems of our land, continues to damage black lives and erode white souls.
>
> (From the Rev. Dr. John Paddock, Rector of Christ Episcopal Church, Dayton, whose son was one of the students on the bus that day.)[43]

Christopher, because you have colleagues who are looking for ways to cope with discrimination in many forms, this gives you insight and empathy. Consider these recommendations.

- Gather a small group of friends for support, discussions, and forming action plans. The Lone Ranger model never goes very far. We need each other in times like these.
- Keep on keeping on caring and praying for your marginalized acquaintances.
- Be informed. Research your areas of concern, especially the Muslim religion. Biased reporting and widespread fear lead to mixed messages and unclear interpretations.
- Remind yourself that you are a Christian and that Christianity has a valid reputation for being countercultural. Perhaps this often-told preacher's story best illustrates serious Christian commitment. Several years ago, an American journalist was assigned the task of reporting on Catholic hospitals in China. One day as he was visiting one of these medical centers, he came across a nun who was cleaning the gangrenous sores of a soldier. The reporter looked at her and commented, "I would not do that for a million dollars." The nun is reported to have continued her work and said, "Neither would I, but for Jesus I would."

These unconventional words of Jesus speak loudly and clearly.

You have heard that it was said to those of ancient times, "You shall not murder'; and 'whoever murders shall be liable to judgement." But I say to you that if you are angry with another, you will be liable to judgement. (Matthew 5:21–22 NRSV)

You have heard it was said, "An eye for an eye and a tooth for a tooth." But I say to you, Do not resist an evildoer. But if anyone strikes you on the right cheek, turn the other also. (Matthew 5:38–39 NRSV)

You have heard that it was said, "You shall love your neighbor and hate your enemy." but I say to you, love your enemies and pray for those who persecute you. (Matthew 5:43–44 NRSV)

To paraphrase the teachings of Jesus, "Yes, I understand your situation, but there is another option. There are ways to break out of your unhealthy, unforgiving, bitter attitudes. There are alternatives in getting unstuck from your painful situation."

Christopher, in responding to your thoughtful, timely inquiry, I tried not to offer you simple answers and easy solutions. I have experienced untold restless nights and anxious days living with and coping with stressful social injustices, while trying to be faithful to Jesus, my family, my church, and my country. I pray that you will not get discouraged, will not standby idly, and will not ask, "What would Jesus do?" Rather, you should ask, "What would Jesus want me to do?"

Granddaddy

Letter 10
Fan or Follower

O God, from my youth you have taught me,
and I still proclaim your wondrous deeds.
So even to old age and gray hairs, O God,
do not forsake me, until I proclaim your might
to all generations to come.
—Psalm 71:17–18 (NRSV)

Christopher,

Your inquiring mind has blessed me immensely. You certainly had some significant questions. However, now I want to ask you one.

Are you a fan or a follower of Jesus?

Before you answer that question, I want to tell you a story. Once upon a time, there was a boy whose parents took him to church to be baptized into the Christian family when he was a baby. As he grew older, he was read Bible stories at home and went to Sunday school each week, as was his family's custom. When the boy turned twelve, he was enrolled in the pastor's Confirmation class. A year later, he took his vows of church membership, and everyone in the congregation applauded s his parents hugged him. As he grew older, he participated in churchly activities and showed up on Sundays almost every week. But was he a fan or a follower of Jesus?

By definition, a fan is an enthusiastic admirer. This is like someone who goes to a football game, cheers wildly for his team, and plays the role of the coach or the quarterback from the viewing stands. He is never in the game. He never breaks a sweat. He never takes a hit. He knows all about the players, but he doesn't know them personally. When the game is over, he goes home and waits until the next game to become once more an enthusiastic fan. But Jesus was never interested in having admiring fans.[44]

A follower by definition is someone personally committed to the leader who gets involved in the day-to-day play action. A follower will volunteer to move out of his or her comfort zone to pursue the mission goals of the leader. A follower personally knows the leader and is willing to make sacrifices.

As I wrote in an earlier letter, Jesus's only requirement when recruiting the disciples is, "Follow me." All four Gospels record this foundational invitation of Jesus. He also issued these instructions: "All who want to come after me must say no to themselves, take up their cross daily, and follow me. All who want to save their lives will lose them. But all who lose their lives because of me will save them" (Luke 9:23–24 CEB).

With such seemingly rigid demands, it makes you wonder why millions of human beings have said yes to Jesus and taken the name Christian. Could it be that in their attempts to be faithful they have discovered blessings unlimited and the abundant life Jesus offers (John 10:10–11 NRSV)?

The only command Jesus gave to his followers turns out to be the key to everyday discipleship: "As the Father has loved me, so have I loved you. These things I have spoken to you, that my joy may be in you, and that your joy may be full. This is my commandment, that you love one another as I have loved you" (John 15:9–12 NRSV).

No doubt this is what Mother Teresa had in mind when a group of tourists were leaving Calcutta one day. As I heard the story, they asked a favor. "Mother Teresa, could you give us a word to take home with us, something that will help us remember our time with you and to be better Christians?" She smiled and said, "Following Jesus faithfully can be very demanding. When that happens, just smile at Jesus, smile at one another, and do what he wants you to do."

Christopher, did anyone ever tell you the significance of your name? It comes from the Greek word *Christophoros*, meaning to bear or to carry Christ. Those who have this given name have the honor of carrying Christ in their hearts. Today, St. Christopher is regarded as the patron saint of travelers, based on a legend from the Middle Ages depicting a man named Christopher who helped carry the young Jesus across a river one day. When you were baptized, the pastor claimed you for Christ and received you into the Christian faith. Because of your baptism, you may serve Christ in whatever line of work or life's pathway you pursue. Of course, you do have a choice in this matter of bearing Christ. Your God-given free will allows you to decide every minute, every hour, and every day whether you will be a fan or a follower.

Let's assume you are motivated to be a serious follower of Jesus Christ. Does he have a specific plan for your life? If he does, how can you access your divinely engineered plan? Is there a pre-birth blueprint awaiting to be discovered, complete with detailed specifications on what to do with your life? I believe this is possible but highly unlikely for multitudes of human beings inhabiting the earth, although the Bible does record certain persons who were preordained for specific kinds of ministries. Check out Jeremiah 1:4 NRSV. "Now the word of the Lord came to Jeremiah saying, 'Before I formed you in the womb I knew you, and before you were born I consecrated you; I appointed you to be a prophet to the nations.'" Jeremiah was only a boy (perhaps a young teenager) at the time he objected to the God's appointment, but he later went on to follow his calling.

I find it interesting that some Christians I have met who attempt to discern God's life path quote Jeremiah 29:11 (NRSV), "For surely I know the plans I have for you, says the Lord, plans for your welfare and not for your harm, to give you a future with hope." The word *plans* in this verse comes from a Hebrew word that can also be translated as "thoughts" or "purpose." Furthermore, notice the verses that follow. "When you call upon me and come and pray to me, I will hear you. When you search for me you will find me, if you seek me with all your heart" (Jeremiah 29:12–13 NRSV).

Do not skip over this required initiative to pray, search, and seek in knowing and discovering God's thoughts or purpose in your life. Also, we need to be aware that God has already given definite instructions or guidelines that we can use and apply in our everyday lives. Jesus highlighted God's yearnings for all human beings when a religious leader asked him, "Which commandment is the first of all." Jesus answered,

> The first is, the Lord our God is one; you shall love the Lord your God with all your heart and with all your soul and with all your mind and with all your strength. The second is this; you shall love your neighbor as yourself. There is no

other commandment greater than these" (Mark 12:28–31 NRSV)

In addition to these priceless and rewarding mandates, we have other trustworthy guidelines; such as the Ten Commandments (Exodus 20:1–17 NRSV), the Book of Psalms, the Sermon on the Mount (Matthew 5–7 NRSV), and the parables of Jesus. God's thoughts and purposes for your life will become clear when you decide to take seriously the timeless and relevant biblical prescriptions already available. As the hymn goes, "Trust and obey, for there is no other way to be happy in Jesus."[45]

The more faithful you are in living God's recorded instructions, the more confidence you will have in being a follower of Jesus in whatever circumstance, situation, line of work, or career path you pursue.

Christopher, here is a legendary story I heard many years ago, and I now pass it on to you. This is about the devil, who was getting ready to move from one part of the world to another area. He had a moving sale to finance his relocation. The devil carefully displayed and priced his inventory—things that could be replaced later. Along came an interested shopper, a man who was surprised at the high price on an item marked "Discouragement." "Tell me why so much money for this?"

"Well, you need to know," responded the devil, "that with the tool of discouragement, I can gain access into unlimited numbers of lives. When people get really discouraged, they are extremely vulnerable to all kinds of negative stuff in my arsenal of temptations."

Being a Jesus follower 100 percent of the time can get discouraging. The term often used to describe this reality is countercultural. The Gospel (good news) Jesus taught and lived has a way of going against much-accepted social behavior and conventional wisdom. We may not be crucified, but we will meet opposition and challenges when we refuse "to go along, to get along," and when our consciences tell us to pay attention to Jesus's way. To assist you in overcoming discouragement and help you be a consistent follower of Jesus, I commend the following.

Top Ten Ways to Follow Jesus

1. **Holy baptism:** Remember your baptism and be thankful. When the pastor received and welcomed you into the Christian faith, along with the baptismal water, loving hands were laid upon you with this prayer, "The Holy Spirit work within you, that being born through water and the Spirit, you may be a faithful disciple of Jesus Christ. Amen.[46]

2. **Holy Communion:** Make regular participation in Holy Communion a priority. Why? Because this worship experience consistently brings Christians into personal contact with Jesus Christ. Each time you come to the Lord's table, you have a unique opportunity to bring your personal joys and sorrows, as well as your insufficiencies to the all-sufficient Christ. Here is an excellent way to experience what Jesus was talking about: "I am the vine, you (followers) are the branches. Those who abide in me and I in them bear much fruit, because apart from me you can do nothing" (John 15:5 NRSV).

3. **Develop a lifelong friendship with Jesus:** Gratefully accept Jesus's offer to be your friend. Deeply reflect on his gracious invitation. "No one has greater love than this, to lay down one's life for one's friends. You are my friends if you do what I command you. I do not call you servants any longer, because the servant does not know what the master is doing; but I have called you friends, because I have made known to you everything I have heard from my Father" (John 15:13–15 NRSV). To grow in your friendship with Jesus, consider these guidelines: spend time with each other; share everything that happens in your life; be honest with your feelings and thoughts; hold nothing back; and learn to enjoy listening, talking, and being silent together.[47]

4. **Swallow a frog:** There is a Native American saying: "When you have to swallow a frog, don't stare at it too long." In other words, don't put off what you need to do, even when it might be unpleasant. Move on with your life. Joining the procrastinators club leads to nowhere!

5. **Hang in there:** We often hear this odd, familiar expression. For most people, the meaning is obvious and worth doing. Doing what? The biblical version of "hang in there" is embedded in scripture verses containing these words: steadfast, patience, endurance, persistence, and persevere. "Let endurance have its full effect, so that you may be mature and complete, lacking in nothing" (James 1:4 NRSV).

6. **Set aside time each day to be alone with God:** Basically, we are spiritual beings created in the image of God (Genesis 1:26). Within our DNA is planted a desire to communicate with our creator; this is called prayer. If we slack off in our prayer life, we are stunting our spiritual growth and shunning our relationship with God. The best time of day or night to spend with God in prayer, meditation, and Bible reading, as well as the best place to do this, is personal preference. For guidance on the practice of private prayer, consult with your pastor. Each day, make prayer a priority—or as Jesus put it, "Pray always and do not lose heart" (Luke 18:1 NRSV).

7. **Live the golden rule:** "In everything do to others as you would have them do to you; for this is the law and the prophets" (Matthew 7:12 NRSV)

8. **Three simple rules:** Do no harm. Do good. Stay in love with God. These three simple rules come from the writings and teachings of John Wesley, founder of the Methodist Church in eighteenth-century England.[48] One sure way to stay in love with God is to have a church home, sharing and participating regularly in the body of Christ.

9. **Cope with temptations:** No one is exempt. Even Jesus had to deal with temptations. Immediately following his baptism (one of his high spiritual moments), Jesus went off in the desert for a forty days and forty nights retreat. During this time, he was tested and tempted mercilessly. However, Jesus overcame three devilishly designed temptations. Notice the last sentence in Luke 4:13 (NRSV). "When the devil had finished every test, he departed from Jesus until another opportune time." Here is a word of help and hope. When we are challenged by temptations, our best line of defense is to call on the name of Jesus quickly, quietly, and repeatedly. Jesus,

who was tempted many times just as we are, stands ready to deliver us from evil.

10. **Remember your name:** Christopher means "the Christ-bearer." Not everyone is blessed with this unique name. However, all who have been baptized bear Christ within their souls and outwardly carry the name Christian. The challenge is to live faithfully and fully into that name. A century ago, the noted humanitarian, theologian, and medical doctor Albert Schweitzer expressed this same quest when he wrote these unforgettable words.

He comes to us as One unknown, without a name, as of old, by the lakeside, He came to those men who knew him not. He speaks to us the same word: "Follow thou me!" and sets us to the tasks which He has to fulfill for our time. He commands. And to those who obey Him, whether they be wise or simple, He will reveal Himself in the toils, the conflicts, the sufferings which they shall pass through in His fellowship, and, as an ineffable (indescribable) mystery, they shall learn in their own experience who He is.[49]

Christopher, let's stay in touch. Call or send an e-mail anytime. I love you, have you in my daily prayers, and know that Jesus Christ, our Lord and Savior, is with you twenty-four seven, eager to help carry your loads, meet your challenges, and shower you with blessings unlimited. I share with you my prayer upon awaking each morning.

Gracious and Loving God, now I rise to greet this day, with desire to follow the Jesus way. Keep me on the path of right and show me how I might share your love and grace with all who see my face. Amen.

Now, the question I posed in the beginning of this letter—one that only you can answer. Are you a fan or a follower of Jesus?

Granddaddy

Epilogue

Memory is truly one of God's most precious and priceless gifts to humanity. In writing *Letters to Christopher,* I was able to recall special people, particular places, and significant events that have shaped and influenced my life's journey these past eighty-plus years. To everyone living in the fourth quarter of life, I highly recommend this reflective exercise. For instance, my homiletics professor at United Theological Seminary, Dr. E. E. Burtner, made a profound statement that sounded good at the time I heard it (1962). I wrote it down, not fully appreciating its deeper meanings.

> Ministers have a God they can't escape, a message they can't hold back, and a people they can't forsake.

I must confess that throughout my years in ministry, there have been moments of indecision, inadequacy, incompetence, and frustration. Yet I did not quit because of my covenant with a God I could not escape, a message I could not hold back, and a people I could not forsake.

Another influential seminary instructor was Dr. Harry DeWire, a professor of pastoral counseling and psychology of religion. One day in class, he wisely pointed out, "What we human beings are looking for in life is a womb with a view." How true! Life in our mothers' wombs was the perfect comfort zone, safe and secure with everything provided. Then came our exit, our day of birth, our entry into an uncomfortable, challenging, and sometimes hostile environment. Not being able to return to the womb, we continuously attempt to substitute and construct other comfort zones: food-filled pantries, clothes closets overflowing, comfortable beds, lodging that is warm in the winter and cool in the summer, money in the bank, many amenities and perceived necessities, and state-of-the-arts television to be our window to all that is happening outside our personal, womb-like existence.

Let it be said that the minister, along with the parsonage family, is not immune to these human wants and wishes that also reside within the church population. We live in constant tension between "back to the womb" ambitions and commitment to Jesus. Here I think about the two apostles who approached Jesus one day with personal requests. Brothers James and John asked him for personal favors. They wanted to sit in the seats of honor to the right and left of Jesus when he came into his future glory. This not only angered the other disciples but also caused Jesus to use that bold request for a teaching moment. "Whoever wishes to become great among you must be your servants ... I came not to be served but to serve" (Mark 10:35–45 NRSV).

Later, when they gathered in that upper room for their last supper, Jesus modeled these instructions by washing the disciples' feet. The four Gospels are quite clear about this. To be serious followers of Jesus, he expects us to deliberately and consciously exit our comfort zones whenever, wherever, and with whomever. My experience is that by preceding and surrounding those anticipated uncomfort zones with prayer, the risen Christ goes with us, ahead of us, and is present with his compassion, grace, and leadership. I regularly call on and rely on his last promise to his disciples before ascending into heaven: "Remember I am with you always, to the end of the age" (Matthew 28:20 NRSV).

Some days I feel as though I have only just begun. In these retired years, my spirit continues to be alert, absorbed, and sensitive to that "something more" God offers every hour of every day.

When I read over some of my earliest sermons and recall many pastoral mistakes I made along the way, I have an urge to start over. But as my wise grandmother put it, "We grow too soon old and too late smart."

My purpose in writing *Letters to Christopher* is not only to highlight our family story but also to pass on what I have learned and am still learning. I also want to encourage others to record their family stories and unique histories. Our life experiences are indelible, not-to-be-forgotten teachers. Let us be generous and honest in sharing what we know to be worthwhile, trustworthy, dependable, and positive. I like the way Richard Rohr expresses this same desire.

> If those of us in my generation do nothing more with the
> rest of our lives than so live that we give hope and meaning

to the next generation, we will have accomplished a great deal. That's what our lives are for: to hand on the mystery to those who are coming after us, which means that we have to appropriate the mystery for ourselves.[50]

So what is this mystery? In several of Paul's letters to New Testament Churches, he lifts up the mystery hidden through the ages but now revealed: "Christ in you, the hope of glory ... I want you to be encouraged and united in love, so that you may have the knowledge of God's mystery, that is Christ himself, in whom is hidden all the treasures of wisdom and knowledge" (Colossians 1:27; Colossians 2:2–3 NRSV). This is the legacy our Christian ancestors gave to us, and now we have the privilege to hand it on to present and future generations.

In closing, I offer a blessing to Christopher and to all the Christophers in the world with this benediction: God loves you just the way you are, but God isn't finished with you yet. Therefore, "may the God of hope fill you with all joy and peace in believing, so that you may abound in hope by the power of the Holy Spirit" (Romans 15:13 NRSV). Amen and amen!

Appendix A
Family Conversations and Videotaping Guide

Does your family have get-togethers for the holidays, family reunions, or special occasions? Mealtimes usually have someone around the table say, "Do you remember when we …?" or, "Tell that story again about …" or, "How did that family tradition ever get started?"

The next time your relatives and in-laws assemble for whatever reason, seriously consider inviting everyone (from the oldest to the youngest) to gather for some relaxed, informal family storytelling. Try this simple plan to preserve and record the conversation.

- Have someone take notes on the highlights, perhaps on a laptop or tablet computer. This could be printed and distributed later to everyone in the family. Better yet, have someone bring a video camera to record the unique voices, faces, and words of the participants.
- One person should act as the facilitator or moderator to keep the discussion flowing, being sensitive to some family members who might be a bit shy in sharing, or gently telling those who tend to dominate the conversation to let others have the floor.

Here is a list of twenty lead-ins that could be used as starters. These are mainly addressed to older family members. However, do not have age-limits. Encourage spontaneous interaction from all who are present.

1. What are some of your earliest memories?
2. Tell us how you got your name.
3. Tell us about your grandparents or great grandparents. Do you remember any stories they told you?

4. Describe your parents or the people who raised you.
5. Say something about the places and memories where you grew up.
6. What experiences do you remember most vividly from your childhood?
7. If you had brothers and sisters, what were their names, and what memories do you have of them?
8. What was school like when you were a child? Can you recall your first day at school, early teachers, and best friends?
9. What difficult or important decisions did you have to make during your early years?
10. What were some of the jobs or occupations you worked during your life? Any stories to recall about your work?
11. In life we often have stories of sadness and trauma. Anything to share here?
12. How and where did you meet your spouse? Any stories about your spouse?
13. Any stories about your relationship with your children? What about children's stories about their parents?
14. For grandparents and grandchildren: tell stories about each other.
15. What do you consider to be the greatest satisfaction or blessing of your life?
16. Is there a favorite family story you have not heard today but want to hear now?
17. What have been some of the most difficult problems or challenges in your life?
18. What are some lessons you've learned from losses or failures?
19. If you could tell your children or grandchildren and those who come after you one thing to remember and to do, what would that be?
20. In one short sentence, summarize your life story.[51]

Because of time constraints, you need to adapt these twenty lead-ins to your family situation, selecting those discussion starters that may produce interesting responses. In large family gatherings, where the conversations flow easily and the highlights are recorded, you can say something like this: "What a wonderful storytelling and sharing time we have had. Perhaps we could continue this when we get together again."

For closure, read these insightful words by John Van DeLaar, a Methodist minister living with his family in South Africa.

> When storykeepers do their work, they give us a sense of dignity, of knowing who we are. Each of us is a product not only of our own life experiences but also of the ancestors who came before us, and of the history they wrote. When we forget the stories of those who came before us, we lose touch with the forces that have shaped and continue to shape us. But, when we make the time to remember the stories of our past, to connect with those who came before us, and to find our place in the ancient history of our people, we know ourselves more deeply, and we learn who we really are.[52]

Appendix B
Small Group Discussion Guide

A small group can be any gathering of people who have a common interest, such as cooking and eating together, book clubs, neighborhood friends, Sunday school classes, or those who meet for Bible study and prayer. *Letters to Christopher* could be used as a springboard for small groups who are interested in sharing their life stories. If group members are open to this possibility, consider these guidelines.

- Distribute copies of *Letters to Christopher* to each group member, to be read privately.
- At the next meeting, invite discussion on the highlights of the book. Then read aloud the following.

  There is in each of us an ongoing story. It contains our meaning and our destiny. This is our "soul-story." Though we do not know its final outcome, nor even what will come tomorrow, there is never-the-less a great joy and peace in knowing we are with the story. This is our soul's journey. This is what life is all about.[53]

- Facilitator: One person could lead each meeting, or group members could take turns leading from session to session.
- Assign dates for each group member to share personal life stories.
- Covenant (agree) to be present for all sessions, to set time limits for each meeting (no less than one hour or more than two), and to come to each meeting with a listening heart and a loving spirit.

Protect the confidentiality of personal stories and group discussions. Here are other options to consider with your group.

- From the twenty lead-in starter questions listed in Appendix A, select those appropriate for your group.
- Use these conversation points related to *Letters to Christopher.*
  - Has anyone ever had a significant coincidence, or a God-incident? Describe it.
  - Relocating from one part of the country to another can be stressful and positive at the same time. Any stories about moving experiences?
  - Discuss personal health topics, such as physical fitness, dieting and body weight issues, doctors, and hospital happenings.
  - Discuss personal expectations in belonging to a church, challenges in changing churches, and other church experiences.
  - Forgiveness and unforgiveness issues are present in everyone's life. Is this a topic some may want to discuss?

1. Reflect on the concept of living your life in four seasons (spring, summer, autumn, winter) or four quarters (ages 1–25, 26–50, 51–75, and 76 and older).
2. Coping with grief and the loss of loved ones: There are no rules or guidelines for grieving. Yet "grief shared is grief divided" (Anonymous).
3. Letter 9, "Fan or Follower," raises the question of what it means to be a seriously committed Christian. Your group might want to discuss "Ten Ways to Follow Jesus."
4. Can the group members relate to this quotation by Wayne Dyer?

   We are not human beings having a spiritual experience.
   We are spiritual beings having a human experience.

5. The author claims, "A good book is good company." Share some positive influences, life-enhancing experiences, and personal enjoyment in keeping company with books.

Closure: Read aloud this encouraging word.

   The process of storytelling is itself a healing process, partly because you have someone there who is taking the time to tell you a story that has meaning for them. They want to give it to you in a form that becomes inseparable from your whole self. That's what stories do. Stories differ from advice in that, once you get them, they become a fabric of your whole soul. That is why they heal you.[54]

Celebrate your story!

Celebrate others' stories!

Celebrate God's story!

Appendix C
Personal Reflections and Remembrances

> Telling the story of our lives is one of the most importantactivities
> of the later years. It reminds us that we are stillemerging, growing
> people. It shows us how we havechanged and how we have
> been transformed. Life reviewis a stabilization in the security
> of the past so that we cango beyond to embrace the future.
> —Jane Marie Thibault[55]

You have a uniquely personal history. Reflecting on your life to recall influential people, memorable events, and personal highlights is much more than a nostalgic exercise. The values include a thankful heart for all your past blessings, courage to keep on keeping on, and undaunted hope for the future. No one is exempt from disappointments, grief, and setbacks.

However, Apostle Paul spoke the truth when he wrote, "We know that all things work together for good for those who love God, who are called according to his purpose" (Romans 8:28 NRSV). Notice Paul does not say that God causes all things to happen. Rather, God is able and willing to use all of your experiences (the good ones as well as the not-so-good ones) in amazing ways when you go with the flow of God's shepherding spirit from day to day. When bad things do happen to good people, the helpful question is not "Why?" but "Now that this has happened, what might be my next step, knowing I can count on God's help?"[56]

Should you decide to record your life-story, here are some suggestions.

1. Do not rush, hurry or try to meet an imaginary deadline. Record various episodes from your personal life whenever you are so motivated. This should be an honest, truthful, and enjoyable experience.

2. To assist in organizing your remembrances, consider dividing your years into time frames. This does not have to be precise, and there may be some overlapping. To get started, jot down significant reflections in each time segment. This can be revised and organized as you move along.

3. Someone has wisely commented: "When you want to be creative, stay close to the Creator." You may find it relaxing and helpful to bathe your journaling efforts in prayer.

4. To assist in jogging your memory bank, review the twenty lead-ins listed in Appendix A and the ten conversation points in Appendix B. Adapt any of these that may be appropriate.

5. As you reflect on your personal history, were there times when restless nights and anxious days seemed to dominate your life? If so, name some of the daunting issues you faced.

6. Upon completing your reflections and remembrances, you may decide to file it all away for future reference, or share what you have recorded with family members and good friends, or consider having your manuscript published.

A prayer of affirmation and hope:

Gracious and loving God, truly like a good shepherd you know me by name. Gently you lead me day after day after day. Even though I do not know what the future holds, I do know you are in my future. Therefore, I can live fully and without fear in the present because your Holy Spirit is with me, loving me, guiding me, empowering me, and healing me through Jesus Christ who is the same yesterday, today, and forever. Amen![57]

Endnotes

1   David Baldacci, *Wish You Well* (New York: Warner Books, Inc, 2000), x.
2   Roland Bainton, *Here I Stand* (Nashville: Abingdon-Cokesbury Press, 1950). It is a definitive and clarifying book on the life and times of Martin Luther.
3   Special note of appreciation to three Presbyterian ministers whose pioneering initiative in Christian healing ministry mentored and inspired countless others to do likewise: Rev. Richard Ellsworth, Central College Presbyterian Church, Westerville, Ohio; Rev. Robert Ward, First United Presbyterian Church, Middletown, Ohio; Rev. Don Bartow, Westminister Presbyterian Church, Canton, Ohio.
4   James Miller, *Hardwired: Finding the God You Already Know* (Nashville: Abingdon Press, 2013).
5   James K. Wagner, *Blessed to Be a Blessing* (Nashville: The Upper Room Books, 1980), 28. The title is taken directly from God's call to Abraham in the Book of Genesis 12:2, "I will bless you so that you will be a blessing."
6   James K. Wagner, *The Spiritual Heart of Your Health* (Nashville: Upper Room Books, 2002), 181.
7   Wagner, *Blessed to Be a Blessing,* 34–35.
8   Ibid., 35.
9   Ibid., 35.
10 Dale A. Matthews, *The Faith Factor: Proof of the Healing Power of Prayer* (New York: Viking Penguin Group, 1998), 15–16.
11 James K. Wagner, *Anna, Jesus Loves You* (Nashville: The Upper Room, 1985), 32–33.
12 Ibid., 105–106.
13 Ibid., 102–103.
14 Albert E. Day, *Discipline and Discovery* (Springdale, PA: Whitaker House, 1988), 11–12.
15 *United Methodist Book of Worship* (Nashville: The United Methodist Publishing House, 1992), 613–614.
16 Albert E. Day, *Letters on the Healing Ministry* (Nashville: The Upper Room, 1990), 7–8.
17 The Disciplined Order of Christ (DOC) is an ecumenical, spiritual renewal movement launched in the summer of 1945 at Albion College, Michigan. For

additional information, contact the DOC National Headquarters, PO Box 3681, Florence, SC 29502, or phone 843-664-2042.

[18] Maxie Dunnam, *Workbook of Spiritual Disciplines* (Nashville: The Upper Room, 1984), 15.

[19] Day, *Discipline and Discovery*, 156.

[20] James K. Wagner, *Forgiveness: The Jesus Way* (Lima, OH: CSS Publishing Company, Inc., 2007), 7.

[21] Ibid., 15.

[22] Ibid., 42+.

[23] See Doris Donnelly in my recommended bibliography.

[24] Op. cit., Wagner, *Forgiveness: The Jesus Way*, 24.

[25] Op. cit., Wagner, *Blessed to Be a Blessing*, 86.

[26] Op. cit., Wagner, *Forgiveness: The Jesus Way*, 33.

[27] Wagner, Ibid., 36–37.

[28] Elton Trueblood, *A Place to Stand* (New York: Harper & Row Publishers, 1969), 38–39.

[29] Op. cit., Wagner, *Blessed to Be a Blessing*, 31–32.

[30] James K. Wagner, *An Adventure in Healing and Wholeness* (Nashville: Upper Room Books, 1993), 106–107.

[31] Ibid., 107.

[32] From a sermon by Oral Roberts in Philadelphia at the Congress on Evangelism of the United Methodist Church in 1976. For further insights on why all people are not healed, see *Blessed to Be a Blessing* by James K. Wagner, chapter 5, "When Healings Do Not Happen."

[33] For an in-depth study and discussion on the crucifixion of Christ, see Tony Jones, *Did God Kill Jesus?* (New York: HarperCollins Publishers, 2015).

[34] Richard Rohr, *Everything Belongs* (New York: Crossroad Publishing Company, 1999), 169.

[35] Leslie Weatherhead, *The Will of God*, edited by Rebecca Laird (Nashville: Abingdon Press, 1995), 25–26.

[36] Richard L. Morgan, *No Wrinkles on the Soul* (Nashville: Upper Room, Books, 2002).

[37] United Methodist Hymnal, *Great Is Thy Faithfulness* (Nashville: The United Methodist Publishing House,1989), No. 140.

[38] The United Methodist Church for All People is an inner-city church in Columbus, Ohio, ministering to a diverse congregation and multiethnic, multicultural community. Training events are regularly scheduled to demonstrate ways to offer this specialized ministry in other places. For additional information, write to 946 Parsons Ave, PO Box 6063 Columbus, OH 43206; phone 614-445-7342; or go online to www.4allpeople.org.

[39] United Methodist Hymnal, No.707.

[40] Sarah Young, *Jesus Calling* (Nashville: Thomas Nelson, Inc. 2011), 309.

41 From a sermon by Dr. Reginald Mallett, presented at Lake Junaluska, NC.

42 Flora Wuellner, *Beyond Death: What Jesus Revealed about Eternal Life* (Nashville: Upper Room Books, 2014), 14.

43 Rev. Dr. John Paddock, "Letter to the Editor," *Dayton Daily News,* Dayton, Ohio (February 11, 2017).

44 Kyle Idleman, *Not a Fan* (Grand Rapids, MI: Zondervan, 2011), 24–25.

45 United Methodist Hymnal, No. 467.

46 *United Methodist Book of Worship,* 98.

47 Trevor Hudson, *Beyond Loneliness: The Gift of God's Friendship* (Nashville: Upper Room Books, 2016), 13.

48 See Rueben Job, *Three Simple Rules* (Nashville: Abingdon Press, 2007), 10.

49 Richard A. Wing, *Finding Your Lambarene* (Columbus, OH: First Community Church, 2011), 34–35.

50 Op. cit., Richard Rohr, *Everything Belongs,* 123.

51 Richard L. Morgan, *Remembering Your Story* (Nashville: Upper Room Books, 1996), adapted from pages 155–156. Also recommended for audiotaping/ videotaping life stories is Bill Zimmerman's book, *How to Tape Instant Oral Biographies* (New York: Guarionex Press, 1994).

52 John Van DeLaar, *Weavings Magazine* 31, no. 3: 17–18.

53 Op. cit., Morgan, *Remembering Your Story,* 140–141.

54 Ibid.,141.

55 Ibid., 28.

56 Op. cit., Wagner, *Adventure in Healing and Wholeness,* 65.

57 Ibid., 69.

Bibliography

Baldacci, David. *Wish You Were Here*. New York: Warner Books, Inc., 2000.

Day, Albert E. *Discipline and Discovery*. Springdale, PA: Whitaker House, 1988.

Day, Albert E. *Letters on the Healing Ministry*. Nashville: The Upper Room, 1990.

Donnelly, Doris. *Learning to Forgive*. Nashville: Abingdon Press, 1979.

Donnelly, Doris. *Putting Forgiveness into Action*. Allen, TX: Argus Communications, 1982.

Hudson, Trevor. *Beyond Loneliness: The Gift of God's Friendship*. Nashville: Upper Room Books, 2016.

Idleman, Kyle. *Not a Fan*. Grand Rapids, MI: Zondervan, 2011.

Job, Rueben. *Three Simple Rules*. Nashville: Abingdon Press, 2007.

Jones, Tony. *Did God Kill Jesus?* New York: HarperCollins Publisher, 2015.

Matthew, Dale A. *The Faith Factor: Positive Proof of the Healing Power of Prayer*. New York: Viking Penquin Group, 1998.

Miller, James W. *Hardwired: Finding the God You Already Know*. Nashville: Abingdon Press, 2013.

Morgan, Richard L. *Remembering Your Story*. Nashville: Upper Room Books, 1996.

Rohr, Richard. *Everything Belongs*. New York: Crossroad Publishing Company, 1999.

Rohr, Richard. *Immortal Diamond*. San Francisco: Josey-Bass, 2013.

Wagner, James K. *An Adventure in Healing and Wholeness*. Nashville: Upper Room, 1993.

_____. *Anna, Jesus Loves You*. Nashville: Upper Room, 1985.

_____. *Blessed to Be a Blessing*. Nashville: Upper Room, 1980.

_____. *Forgiveness: The Jesus Way*. Lima, OH: CSS Publishing Co., 2007.

_____. *Healing Services*. Nashville: Abingdon Press, 2007.

_____. *The Spiritual Heart of Your Health*. Nashville: Upper Room Books, 2002.

Weatherhead, Leslie. *God's Will: A Workbook*. Edited by Rebecca Laird. Nashville: Abingdon Press, 1995.

Wing, Richard A. *Finding Your Lambarene*. Columbus, OH: First Community Church, 2011.

Wuellner, Flora. *Beyond Death: What Jesus Revealed about Eternal Life*. Nashville: Upper Room Books, 2014.

Young, Sarah. *Jesus Calling*. Nashville: Thomas Nelson, Inc., 2011.

Printed in the United States
By Bookmasters